MW01717043

THE ROBIN HOOD of D.C.

Joe Kuklis

Published by Charles Pinot

First Printing, 2012
10 9 8 7 6 5 4 3 2 1

Copyright © 2012 Charles Pinot. All rights reserved. Printed in the United States of America. No part of this publication may be reproduced or distributed in any form or by any means, or stored in a database or retrieval system, except as permitted under Sections 107 or 108 of the U.S. Copyright Act, without prior written permission of the publisher. This book is printed on acid free paper.

Material in this book is for educational purposes only. This product is sold with the understanding that neither any of the authors nor the publisher are engaged in rendering legal, accounting, investment, or any other professional service specifically suited to one particular individual's needs who may be reading this book. Neither the publisher nor the authors assume any liability for any errors or omissions or for how this book or its contents are used or interpreted or for any consequences resulting directly or indirectly from the use of this book.

The views expressed by the individuals in this book do not necessarily reflect the views shared by the companies they are employed by (or the companies mentioned in this book). The employment status and affiliations of the authors with the companies referenced are subject to change.

The Robin Hood of D.C.

Table of Contents

DEDICATIONS

I would be remiss if I didn't take the time to thank everyone that has made this opportunity possible for me. Many friends, family and colleagues helped me to aspire and live my dreams of entrepreneurship and public service. This book memorializes much of that journey until now, and I owe them a debt of humbled gratitude as they, each in their own way, allowed me to achieve many of my personal goals.

To my wife, Andrea, I simply say "thank you." You have always been there for me, through thick and thin, and have taken on many responsibilities in our private life that should be shared more equally, including bearing many crosses that are not of your making;

To my mother, Jackie, who showed me the path to success is not always counted by the value of a bank account, but by the fulfillment and happiness of your personal life. One of my best friends, Adam Gyurisin, once said to me "that's not how it is in my book, and my book is the only one that counts." Mom, you are the definition and epitome of that statement;

To my Uncle Joe who, from his wheelchair and his bedroom, inspired me from a young age and sparked my interest in authorship. He taught me so many lessons that helped shape the decisions I made in my life before he left us all too early. His wounds in Vietnam may have cut his life too short, but his values and courage live on in these words;

To my brother Dave who, without his support and sacrifice, I would not be able to lead the life I live. I admire you in so many ways, and that is difficult for an older brother to admit. For this I am eternally grateful;

To my mentor, Senator Rick Santorum, for without his guidance in the early part of my career, I would not have been able to achieve success in public service or in entrepreneurship. Time spent serving the constituents of Pennsylvania with him taught me many of the ideals and philosophies that have made my endeavors successful. It was the opportunity he gave me that made this all possible;

To my business partners over the years – John Dick, Amy Kaminski, Aaron Grau, Tom Beresnyak, Alyssa Kunselman, Kim Hileman, Shawn Good, Pat Stewart, Ted Christian and Eric Martins. Without your faith in me, your commitment to GSP and DMGS, and your trust, our success would not be possible.

To those fellow entrepreneurs who understand what it takes to start and run a business, thanks for imparting the wisdom gained through your own experiences and for supporting a kindred spirit;

And finally to those who thought we couldn't do it, told us we couldn't do it and tried to stop us from doing it - thanks for the motivation and the locker room bulletin board material.

INTRODUCTION

In its simplest form, political lobbying is the process of influencing public and government policy at all levels: federal, state and local. As a critical function in the government process, lobbying is a necessary element when seeking to navigate the government marketplace.

Lobbying, which is protected by the First Amendment, is considered essential to the proper functioning of government because it provides a forum for conflict resolution among views that are often diverse or competing; provides information, analysis, and opinion to legislators and government leaders to allow for informed and balanced decision making; and creates a system of checks and balances that allows for competition among interest groups, keeping any one group from attaining a permanent position of power. Lobbyists can help the legislative process work more effectively by providing lawmakers with reliable data and accurate assessments of a bill's effect.

This may all sound simple, and yet most people, unless directly involved in lobbying of some sort, have only a vague notion of what lobbying is, what it entails, and the good it can do. If you are one of those people, let me show you by way of example the immense power of political lobbying.

Austin's Playrooms

Let me illustrate the point above with an unorthodox example of how lobbyists "bolt on" to your operation and guide you through the labyrinth of the government maze.

At GSP and now Duane Morris Government Strategies (DMGS), our business helps organizations and companies find the money to fund the projects and initiatives, the moves and expansions that are integral to helping them grow and thrive. For the Pittsburgh-based Mario Lemieux Foundation, we assist them by identifying and securing critical funding to help both kids and their parents with the development of a program named after Mario's son, Austin.

Here in Pittsburgh, you don't need to be a hockey fan to know the name Mario Lemieux. A Hall of Fame National Hockey League player and co-owner of the Pittsburgh Penguins, Mario is an icon in our fair city. Over the years, GSP worked with a wide variety of clients and when one thinks about a lobbyist, the image they conjure in their heads rarely pairs a sports figure retaining the services of a firm like ours. However, GSP's portfolio extends to groups such as the Mario Lemieux Foundation, helping them fulfill their philanthropic mission in the community.

The concept behind the Austin's Playroom program came from a personal experience of Mario and his wife, Nathalie. Mario was on a road trip during the long NHL season and Nathalie was in Pittsburgh with their children. Their son, Austin was born prematurely and had subsequent health issues in his younger years. One of those trips to the local hospital took Nathalie to an emergency room in the early hours of the morning with Austin's other siblings in tow. When Nathalie was presented with the idea of having to either leave her daughters in the waiting room unattended to be with her son – or, leave her son with the doctors for treatment while staying back with her daughters – the idea for Austin's Playrooms was born.

The concept here was simple – build out space in hospitals for kids to be left safely (and in some cases with supervision) so that parents can be with an ailing child. The rooms could also double during the day as playrooms in hospitals for kids outside of their traditional hospital beds. The foundation developed the program and began to raise money for the construction of Austin's Playrooms in several local hospitals. When the first few were complete, other area hospitals started to look at adopting the same concept and the foundation realized they were on to something special.

The success of the first few playrooms spawned the idea to build more and the idea to seek public funding to help launch more playrooms reached our door through the foundation's Executive Director, Nancy Angus. The foundation and hospital community had identified a need that could, in part, be filled with grants from federal or state sources. Many federal departments and agencies have funding for projects that promote better public health, community development, hospital renovations and the like. GSP was retained by the foundation to seek and match public funds, leveraging their privately raised dollars to build more playrooms in hospitals across Pennsylvania. And that's exactly what we did.

Today, the playrooms are a huge success and it's just incredible to walk into any of the Austin's Playroom's hospitals and see the positive effect they have. When a new playroom is opened often the legislators and/or department administrators who were involved in the process are invited to the ribbon cutting ceremony and get to see what a difference they are making in the lives of countless families and how, with their funding, they have been able to make their community a better place to live. It's a great feeling to know you've accomplished something so vital through the power of lobbying.

Today, we still work to obtain state and federal money for the Mario Lemieux Foundation. The main objective of the foundation is to fund promising medical research projects that are conducted by top-notch scientists. The foundation supports grants in cancer research as well as neonatal research. Among the donations made by the foundation was a $5 million gift to the University of Pittsburgh Medical Center to the Mario Lemieux Centers for Patient Care and Research in 2001, and a $2 million gift to the Children's Home of Pittsburgh in 2005.

The funding we secure is allocated across various programs within the foundation, as well as used to fund research efforts that are coordinated by the foundation. To date, we've helped secure more than $200,000 in federal funding for cancer research and several hundred thousand in Pennsylvania-based grants for the Playroom projects. We have also helped the foundation establish a working relationship with the U.S. Department of Defense and its Wounded Warrior program to allow veterans returning from war to visit in similar "playrooms" with their children and family as their struggle to return to a normal life after serious injuries sustained in combat. Recovery for these brave men and women is often a long and arduous process and this new venture from the foundation serves this noble and worthy cause.

The work we've done for the Mario Lemieux Foundation is just one example of what we – or any lobbyist worth his or her salt – can do for your company or organization. And while we've worked with giants like Coca Cola and tiny one-man shops, our niche is helping small- to mid-sized companies and organizations find the money they need to succeed. So whether you want to hire a lobbyist to help on a project or learn to navigate the government ropes yourself, let this book be your guide to your own personal success.

CHAPTER ONE:

Sticks and Stones

Early in my career as a lobbyist, a colleague derogatorily called me the "Robin Hood of D.C." He meant it as an insult. I took it as a compliment, and it's the basis for this book. The story behind the insult is worth recanting so one can appreciate why it was said and why the creation of GSP and our business model was disruptive enough in our marketplace to illicit the remark.

To set the stage, I have to take you back to February of 2001 when my business partner, John Dick, and I started GSP. We had both worked for U.S. Senator Rick Santorum for a number of years. I served on his Congressional and Senatorial staff from 1994 to 2000, and John had just come off the Senator's successful 2000 re-election campaign. During the final stretch of the campaign, John and I knew that, outside of an unforeseen political debacle, the Senator would go back to Washington, and we both knew it was time for us to move on to the next phases of our careers.

I was 28 years old and John was 25, and we both held ambitions of becoming entrepreneurs. In the early 2000s just as the new economy had peaked, John and I both saw young entrepreneurship embraced by the tech and venture communities, and we both saw an opportunity to form a new business to help some of those young tech companies grow and succeed.

I was the Senator's Pennsylvania State Director and was responsible for overseeing the Senator's economic and community development efforts across the state. In that position I had been lobbied in some form or fashion for nearly six years by professional and amateur lobbyists alike and experienced the good, the bad and the ugly of the business.

To be specific, as a representative of a U.S. Senator, I, on a daily basis, would enter into meetings with municipalities, small businesses, community groups and similar organizations that all had government needs but couldn't afford the prices that K Street demanded for representation. I would have municipalities approach me to help them with federal grants for worthy projects like interchanges, brownfield reclamation, parking facilities, the establishment of parks or some other project that held tremendous public benefit.

On the for-profit side, I was just as frequently approached by startup companies that had a technology that could "provide for the common defense or promote the general welfare" but they themselves couldn't get audiences with the right people at federal agencies. Unfortunately, these small- to medium-sized businesses went underserved and underrepresented because they, too, couldn't pay the freight for a D.C.-based lobbyist.

In 1999 and 2000, as the tech bubble began to burst, I saw a spike of activity from tech firms looking for help from the Senator that needed to turn to government as an alternative marketplace for selling their products and services. In some cases, they sought government investment in the form of research and development funding since the traditional venture and angel investments they coveted had all but dried up.

Thankfully, the Senator's office, through its constituent service outreach, provided them with direction, access and support. As State Director, my job was to match make for Pennsylvania companies and organizations with D.C. officials in order for them to present their ideas and products to agency officials that they couldn't reach without us. In some instances, I helped these groups to present policy arguments in front of pertinent Congressional staff or sitting committees that held oversight to their initiatives or industries.

My time on the Hill revealed to me these weaknesses in the current traditional business model of the average lobbying shop and it dictated to me the new market waiting for representation. Small- to medium-sized organizations of all shapes and sizes needed help, and they couldn't afford to buy the help that was out there. If we could create a company to "serve the underserved" and find a way to make money by doing it, we would have a virtually unlimited pool of potential clients that our competition didn't want to chase.

John's view was very similar but he came at it from a different angle, because his role with the Senator was on the campaign as his Business Coalitions Director. Business Coalitions Director is "campaign code" for raising dollars from various industry groups that support the Senator's views on business issues. He experienced similar angst from companies he approached with regard to their needs in D.C. and their fear of the perceived barriers to entry. Bottom line was they wanted to approach government for help for the first time but were afraid.

When John and I discussed this over many long nights and even more beer, we knew that we had established the basis for our new company – GSP Consulting. We needed to create a company that would cater to the underserved or those that weren't served at all. When we introduced GSP to the marketplace, many of our competitors looked down their nose at our attempt to serve a group of clients too poor or too risky for them to expend their political capital to help.

But as GSP grew in its success and began to grow this new marketplace, our competitors saw it as "robbing from the rich and giving to the poor." It is no coincidence that the back-handed compliment — being called the "Robin Hood of D.C." — was so profound. In the end, they were right. We were the Robin Hoods, helping those who couldn't help themselves.

Hotbed of History

The political process has always fascinated me. Combined with the rich history in and around Pittsburgh and daily doses of the kids' television short, "Schoolhouse Rock," I was hooked from an early age. My first dalliance with politics wasn't very successful however. In elementary school my class was asked to cast a mock vote for President in the 1980 election cycle featuring Carter, Reagan and Anderson. Of my 30 or so classmates, two of us voted for Reagan. Even though Dutch went on to win in the fall, my personal attempts at lobbying my classmates to rally votes for Reagan came up woefully short.

My second attempt at politics came when my third grade teacher, Mrs. Remp, convinced me to run for class president. She knew of my aptitude for politics and thought this was the way to satisfy my interests. Alas, after making my own campaign signs for class president and giving a speech in front of my third-grade peers asking for their votes, I came up short again.

These instances of failure only motivated me to pursue my interests in the art of politics further. Throughout my middle and high school career I enjoyed every civics and history class I could take and even once got sent to the principal's office for "being too exercised in my argument" with my 11th grade American history teacher over the debate question of who was the greater founding father – Alexander Hamilton or Thomas Jefferson? Clearly it was Hamilton and even though in my own mind I won the debate, I lost the war when I had to pay a visit to the principal's office and be scolded for my "outburst."

As a student, however, I excelled in math and science and was pushed by peers and guidance counselors in the direction of engineering when I entered college. During my freshman year, my roommate at the University of Pittsburgh, Dan Lewis, immediately saw the mistake I was making and started "lobbying" me to switch majors. Dan himself was a political science and history major and he and I were incredibly similar. After meeting Dan on more than several occasions, my mom quipped that the only difference between the two of us was that Dan was two years older and I was a half-foot taller.

His read on my choice of majors ended up being incredibly accurate. Coupled with the fact that my freshman year coincided with a historically pivotal time – the fall of the Berlin Wall – Dan harangued me day and night about being part of something special. He saw my interest in the events of the day and encouraged me to chart a different path.

I didn't listen right away, or at least I didn't let on like I was listening. But Dan was right. He could tell my heart was not into the physics or chemistry homework first year engineering students are burdened with, but instead he saw me turning from my desk to join him in watching the news and engaging in healthy political debates. I have to admit, this is when I knew I needed to make a change, and in my sophomore year, I switched majors to political science and also pursued a certificate in Western European Studies with a concentration in the German language and German government. It took me an extra year-and-a-half to graduate, but I am eternally grateful to Dan for helping me understand where my heart truly lay. Of course I never looked back because now, I was completely captivated by the world of politics.

With graduation looming, it was time to decide what I wanted to do when I finished school. In the political world, there are typically four basic options for guys like me: run for office (which is typically something one does later in life), work on someone's campaign, become a lobbyist, or work on Capitol Hill. I chose to work on the Hill, at first as an intern for then-Congressman Rick Santorum. Rick would shortly move on to become Senator Rick Santorum in 1994.

At first, my career started just like many in this field, as unpaid help. Internships are often used to fulfill college credits or to earn your way onto staff in a Congressional office by putting in the required downtime in order to make an impression and learn the routine. However, Congressional staffs turn over very frequently, so a good intern is often seen as farm team material. If you make yourself a useful part of the operation, there is a chance that an offer eventually comes. In my case, it came when Congressman Santorum won election to the U.S. Senate in 1994 and with that victory, the size of his congressional staff doubled.

My first job wasn't sexy and it didn't pay much. My daily experience was comprised of assisting Congressman Santorum in his Whitehall, Pennsylvania district office. My routine consisted of spot duties such as answering phones, providing constituent service work, processing responses to constituent inquiries and driving the Congressman from event to event.

The work may sound boring but it was experiential. I liken that time in my career to the Karate Kid movie when Daniel didn't know why Mr. Miyagi was asking him to paint the fence or sand the floor, but one day it all just kind of came together. That happened for me as I slowly climbed the ranks of his office from intern to front desk help, from front desk help to constituent caseworker, from caseworker to military and veteran affairs coordinator, from military work to Economic & Community Development Director and from there to finally State Director.

Work in a Congressional office isn't the easiest life but it is incredibly rewarding. Yes, 60-hour weeks are common and no, big salaries are not. My first salary was $13,000 (American) and my first two raises did not get me above the poverty line. But I wasn't in it for the money. I was in it for the game.

The career of a congressional staffer is hard to explain. It's a lifestyle job. You don't punch a clock, as you are never really off duty. You can be at a family picnic, a summer carnival or watching a sporting event and invariably someone will ask about your boss's latest vote, your thoughts on the latest presidential polls or complain about some current event.

I didn't blame them for it. Congressional staff jobs are rare and quickly become a centerpiece of any conversation, especially if you work for a Member of Congress who is in leadership or is outspoken on issues. For me, it was both.

People would indulge in the opportunity to tell me their position on a bill or ask for insider information that I couldn't provide on what was "really happening" in the world of U.S. politics. But I didn't mind. That's what I wanted to do in the early part of my career.

The really crazy anecdotes I will save for private ears, but you can imagine some of the questions and comments that are generated from these conversations. When you are in a family of Democrats (save for one brother), the Independence Day family picnic debates could get a little heated.

One of my favorite stories in this regard came from my first date with my future wife, Andrea. I was 22, and she was 21 and living with her parents at the time. I arrived at her house to pick her up and, of course, she wasn't ready. I knew at that point I'd be forced into the awkward conversation with the parents while I waited, but on a first date, I thought for sure they would go easy on me.

As I knocked on the door, her dad answered and politely asked me to come in and join him and his wife while I waited. We struck up the usual conversation that parents and suitors may have the first time you meet — so what's your name, where do you live, and the inevitable, what do you do?

For me, this was a great question. I was still young but I worked for a Congressman. I was sure they wouldn't be expecting to hear that. Perhaps they would expect the usual answers of "I am a full-time student" or "I am in school but working part-time at the library." I knew I could impress them when I hit them with this news.

"I work for Congressman Santorum," I boasted proudly.

A hush fell over the kitchen that I knew was bad, bad news. Much to my chagrin I learned the hard way that her father was a member of the International Brotherhood of Electrical Workers local union and her mother was a former Democratic Committeewoman in their community.

I just remember her mother leaning around the corner, and in a stoic but forceful voice muttering the words, "the man's a pig."

That wasn't the best way to start off a relationship with my future in-laws, but over the years we have thankfully found neutral ground on many a political issue.

Epiphany

The real value one derives from working for a pittance on Capitol Hill is a giant Rolodex of contacts. In the political game of D.C., or any state capitol for that matter, one's network is the lifeblood of his or her trade. Your network is what influences the outcomes of lobbying efforts for your clients, where you find support for friendly legislators for fundraising efforts and where you find new leads for client sales.

So even though I wasn't making a respectable salary like many of my engineering friends did straight out of the college gate, between the ages of 24 and 26, I was building that Rolodex by working with the CEOs of Fortune 500 companies on projects of import to them or lending a hand to presidents of colleges in Pennsylvania for grants. The Hill is blessed with many sharp young minds that help their Members of Congress make decisions on policy issues, appropriations and grants that were available to their constituents. For me, this was the time when I learned my trade and saw the opportunities that existed to create a successful business in this industry.

As I mentioned, lobbying in its simplest form is influencing public and government opinion, or getting someone to see things from your point of view and understanding why that point of view is important. The true "light bulb moment" for me occurred when I realized that I could literally switch sides of the table – to go from working ON the Hill to WORKING the Hill. In doing so, I could create a business and fulfill a lifelong dream of entrepreneurship in a professional field I loved.

The plan was two-fold. First, I needed to build a different kind of lobbying shop. Second, this new company needed to be one that focused on helping a different kind of client, one that hadn't been traditionally served by the competitors that currently existed in the marketplace.

During my time on the Hill, it became evident who my target market would be and where the clients were – those small- to medium-sized organizations that had virtually gone unrepresented in my future business. But the questions remained as to how to build the better mousetrap? How does one build a new business model in an established industry with a brand new client base that in the past had largely been ignored by our competitors?

The answer was simple. We needed to design a company to cater to the needs of this sector by offering them a variety of options to encourage them to buy. The first ingredient in the recipe of GSP's secret sauce was more of a mission statement — we had to give our clients a more responsible price point with more "TLC."

When I was on the Hill, I would hear stories from constituents about how their lobbyists were poorly serving their needs. The usual complaints that resonated with me were tales of the client paying for representation that wouldn't call them back, their representation's fees being too burdensome or their lobbyists carrying conflicting client interests to the Hill. I knew this was the code we needed to break.

In order to accomplish this, our business model had to be different. We needed to provide clients with an affordable service but also be more available to them. We did this by inverting the traditional model of a lobbying shop that was located in the Capitol and instead we set up shop in the cities where our clients were. In the beginning this meant we needed to establish GSP physically in Pittsburgh and once we started to grow, replicate this in cities such as Philadelphia, Cleveland and beyond. Eventually GSP established offices in 11 other cities scattered in a half dozen states.

This didn't mean we ignored the Capitol as we eventually expanded appreciably in D.C. and several state capitols. But by focusing growth in the cities where our clients were, we were able to offer the TLC our clients needed, knowing that we were never far away. This translated into fewer overhead costs for us and our clients. By saving money in avoiding the high rents often associated with Capitol Hill real estate markets, we were able to offer a more competitive price point.

This also worked for GSP as we took on expenses and cost of living for employees that were markedly lower in cities like Pittsburgh and Cleveland. And when we did eventually take office space in D.C., we didn't have $100 a square foot space overlooking the Capitol. Instead we had more reasonable space above the Capitol Lounge, overlooking a bar on Pennsylvania Avenue. This is but one example of ways we were able to cut overhead costs and make our prices fit the market we were chasing.

The second ingredient in our recipe for success focused on providing our clients with a higher level of service than our competition. By listening to folks complain to me about how they needed to hire two lobbyists – one in D.C. and one in their state capitol – we decided to build a company with staff that could handle both federal and state issues. By accomplishing this, GSP served client interests concurrently in both D.C. and Harrisburg.

This is atypical in our industry as many lobbyists are specialists in federal or state affairs and rarely both. But GSP built its team around lobbyists that had experience at working client matters in both D.C. and state capitols.

This was incredibly important to our clients as they now could pay one fee at two-thirds the typical cost for service at two different levels of government. Big savings. More efficiency. Better service.

In addition to the competitive advantage we gained by offering this dual service, the client also enjoyed an unexpected side benefit – continuity. Within the GSP model, our internal state lobbyists and federal lobbyists willingly and thoughtfully exchanged information about efforts for clients. Having both D.C. and state-level work coordinated internally at one shop allowed for a level of alacrity rarely found in our industry.

Often when a prospective client would hire a competitor in D.C. and a different one in a state capitol, usually the two shops wouldn't talk to one another (or when they did, they did begrudgingly). Let's face it - competitors often don't like to share trade secrets, let alone clients. In many cases, there is a level of disinterest from the lobbyist in D.C. in the machinations in places like Harrisburg, Trenton, or Columbus. Same holds true for the state lobbyist that may be indifferent to a client's effort in D.C. Under our business model, the two sides worked together to the client's benefit.

Coupling this strategy with the age-old mantra that the most successful lobbyists are elected officials themselves, we were able to put state and local officials to work for our clients in D.C. and vice versa. In the end, elected officials are chosen to represent their districts or states. To ignore their value in lobbying one level of government to another is a cardinal sin. So by asking our state lobbyists to gather letters of support or calls from state legislators to weigh in on federal issues many times proved fruitful to our efforts for clients.

For example, a letter of support from a state senator for a federal grant can move federal legislators to help more than they may have knowing that it is harder to say "no" to a state senator who asks for support than it is to say "yes". Under the GSP way, our staffers could readily make this work for our clients through the synergy of our combined federal and state teams.

When this model of "more responsible price points meets higher levels of service" was successfully introduced to the marketplace, GSP quickly became an alternative to those who couldn't afford to play in the government world. Over time, the business model started to turn the heads of those companies that had been engaging the more traditional lobbyists because they themselves had to ask the question of whether the GSP way was a better way than what they had been retaining.

If the first part of the epiphany focused on the "how," the second part needed to focus on the "who."

The "who" was obvious to us – it was the underrepresented groups populated by startup technology companies. These businesses were looking for help with federal research funding to advance their new technologies or identify government departments and agencies willing to buy the next generation technology to fill their needs.

In the beginning, John and I decided to pick one of our target industries, small- to medium-sized technology companies, as our focus. We felt that if we branded ourselves as the technology lobbyists, we could dominate this marketplace. The hope was that in the technology community, CEOs, investors, researchers and collaborators were all only one or two degrees of separation from one another, and if we did well for one company, their board of directors, investors and similar interested parties would welcome a referral to their next investment.

As I watched the tech bubble burst, all of the companies that had stayed away from working with government – because of the perceived notion that it just grinds too slowly and the barriers to entry are too high – started to need help. With venture capital having dried up with the recession, these same companies were clambering for a piece of the government pie, but were being stonewalled by their lack of understanding of how to make government work for them without its being an impediment.

We made the decision to focus on the tech community and, in doing so, started to market the company in that direction. The name GSP Consulting was chosen with this target market in mind. We knew that the new economy companies already identified with the ubiquitous terminology of ISPs (Internet service providers) and ASPs (application service providers). We found it clever to call our new service a GSP (government service provider).

The term was a blessing and a curse. Sure it was clever and many of the companies we pitched got the inference. But as the Gods of Irony would have it (and neither John nor I being marketing people), we decided that our first "tagline" for GSP was "Navigating the Government Marketplace."

So in a world of technologists, GSP was often referred to erroneously as "GPS" Consulting. Looking back at it today, it's a funny sidebar and I can't blame anyone for making the mistake. But for the first few years, every time someone would call us "GPS" we could only grin and bear it.

However, the decision for GSP to focus on the technology community turned out to be the right strategic play and the company grew its tech portfolio quickly.

One of my favorite examples was an early conversation I had with Glen Meakem, then the young CEO and founder of FreeMarkets, a Pittsburgh-based Internet company and one of the most successful IPOs in history. In 2001, flush with public market capital and entirely unrepresented in Harrisburg or Washington, FreeMarkets was coveted by every lobbying firm in the market.

John and I were introduced to Glen by a mutual friend, Mark DeSantis. DeSantis, another fellow (and serial) entrepreneur, was consulting for FreeMarkets at the time. Leaning on that friendship, John and I got our day in court with Glen. Both John and I knew that this was the kind of meeting where we would only have only one shot to make an impression. I figured we had little chance of winning the business, considering the caliber of firms with which we were competing.

But the funniest thing happened. Before that meeting ended, Glen, as most brilliant leaders do, quickly and assertively made up his mind. They were going to hire us, he said because he knew what it was like to be in our position. He understood that FreeMarkets could be our biggest and most important early customer. He knew we would give them our absolute "A-Game" because failure was not an option. He was right. We signed the business, served them faithfully for years, and Glen developed into one of our most valued mentors in the process.

I look back at this as one of those pivotal moments in our start-up phase, not so much because it brought a big retainer that helped pay the bills (though it really, really did) but because everyone in the marketplace, both the lobbying firms and the government community, were stunned that we had landed the whale.

A funny side story came a few months later when we were meeting with another, more established lobbying firm about the possibility of collaborating on a project. One of the principals pulled me aside after the meeting and said, "You guys have a great little niche with these small start-ups and non-profit clients. Why don't you let us handle your FreeMarkets account? It might be a little over your head."

"Sure," I said, "Should I have them mail the retainer check to your Pittsburgh or Harrisburg office?" Of course, that's not at all what I said. It's just that my real response isn't fit for print in a book like this.

The BIG Win/David vs. Goliath

While winning the FreeMarkets business was a huge moment for GSP, our biggest win actually came a few months earlier. Every company needs that one watershed moment or case study that puts them over the hump, and this was ours. Through oddly similar circumstances, this success story owed heavily to the support of other entrepreneurs both in the private AND public sectors.

Early in 2001, then Pennsylvania Governor Tom Ridge announced the creation of the Pennsylvania Tobacco Settlement Investment Board, an organization tasked with administering over $1 billion in capital awarded to the Commonwealth through the federal government's class action lawsuit against tobacco companies. Included in Governor Ridge's plan was a series of programs aimed at fostering investment in early-stage life sciences companies in Pennsylvania. Among these programs was an initiative to deploy up to $60 million of investment capital into three venture capital funds, one each for the eastern, western and central regions of the state.

Smelling that kind of money in the air, every lobbyist in Pennsylvania was jockeying to represent one of the state's indigenous venture capital firms. The conventional wisdom was that it would be much easier to succeed for a fund with a history of investing locally and with a cadre of wealthy and influential executives who could bring their own local political clout to the table. In Pittsburgh, there was one blue-chip venture fund that fit this mold in spades, and they were quickly snatched up by the biggest lobbying firm in the market.

Through some good friends in the Pittsburgh technology community, we caught wind of a Boston-based venture firm who was quietly assembling a management team to raise a life sciences fund in Pittsburgh. Saturn Asset Management, run by Jeff McCormick, had recruited a marquee managing director for what would become Saturn Life Science Partners ("SLSP") and was actively raising money from local institutional investors. (In an ironic and completely coincidental twist, Saturn Asset Management's lone Pittsburgh investment had come a few years earlier, as the first venture money in FreeMarkets.)

John knew the new managing director of SLSP personally and was able to get us an audience with Jeff McCormick to pitch them on the idea of first chasing the Tobacco Settlement money and, second, choosing us to represent them in their quest. Meeting over lunch on a rainy Monday afternoon, the conversation had a bizarre déjà vu quality to it.

As an experienced entrepreneur-turned-venture-capitalist, Jeff was quick to understand our plight as a start-up firm. "You only need one or two clients like us to make your business work," I remember Jeff saying. "We can put you on the map if we win this thing."

After spending two hours convincing Jeff of our passion, commitment and our strategy, he reached across the table, shook our hands, and uttered any salesman's favorite words, "Send me a contract." Game on.

What most people don't realize about a lobbying initiative like the Tobacco Settlement investment is that the game starts long before the selection committee hears presentations from the competing funds. First, we had to work with the legislature to ensure that the rules and criteria were designed in a way to be favorable to our client. John got to work on that right away, drafting proposed language that allowed an out-of-state fund to be eligible. We also worked to guide the "matching funds" requirements so that they were reasonable given Saturn's fundraising strategy.

Next, we had to develop a plan for affecting the actual composition of the fund selection committee. Each of the four legislative caucus leaders in Harrisburg would appoint one member to the selection committee, in addition to other administrative appointments and at-large members. We needed as many champions on that committee as possible, particularly a few from the western part of the state.

As we scanned the landscape yet again, a fellow entrepreneur came to our aide. John Maher was one of the senior Republican House members in western Pennsylvania and was widely known as his caucus's resident expert on business and finance matters. This distinction resulted from his work in a past life as the founder and principal of a successful accounting firm in Pittsburgh. More importantly, Representative Maher had the ear of the House GOP leadership. If we could get Maher on our side, we had the foundation of support we needed.

In the summer of 2001, John and I met with Representative Maher in his suburban district office and made our case for Saturn – why Pittsburgh would benefit from bringing an out-of-state fund into the region, and why it was worth his time and effort to get involved. He never said so but I will always believe that Maher was moved by our presentation because, as a former entrepreneur, he saw something of himself in us, two scrappy start-up entrepreneurs fighting to build a business against difficult odds. Maher vowed his support, helped us plot the roadmap to victory, and ultimately received the House Republicans' appointment to the fund selection committee.

With an anchor supporter on the committee, we were now able to focus our attention on leveling the playing field with the other caucus and administrative appointees. Our biggest competition in Pittsburgh had tremendous resources at their disposal both financially and through the political muscle of their executives and friends. We needed to neutralize that influence. If Saturn could be evaluated based purely on the merits of their track record and investment strategy, we would win, hands-down.

Over the next year, we launched a campaign of dozens of face-to-face meetings, letters and calls of support, public relations tactics, and overall coalition building. To the outside world, the victory for the bigger, more powerful fund was *fait accompli*. Meanwhile, our confidence grew stronger by the day.

On September 16, 2002, the Pennsylvania Tobacco Settlement Investment Board selected Saturn Life Science Partners, by a committee vote of 10 to 1, to manage $20 million for western Pennsylvania. When the press announcement hit the local papers, you could almost hear jaws hitting the floor all over Pittsburgh. Game over.

Shortly after the announcement, I had one of those moments that bolsters your faith in the world. After a contentious competition with the other Pittsburgh fund, a competition that even bordered on mean and malicious at times, I assumed we had made a long list of mortal enemies. But instead, we started getting calls from the very people we had fought against for nearly 18 months. Successful entrepreneurs and venture capitalists themselves, they respected the way we did our jobs and now wanted to work with us on other projects. Just 31 at the time, I still had a lot to learn.

Growing the Business Model

After being in business for a year, it was evident that the technology community wasn't the only market segment that needed our support. We knew from inception that non-profit organizations of all shapes and sizes could use a group like ours. GSP took the initiative then to begin marketing similar services to a variety of groups such as municipalities, colleges, universities, research institutions, amenity-related non-profits like symphonies, conservatories, tourism groups and economic development agencies. Many of these organizations needed support because they didn't have the internal capacity to handle government-related functions like grant identification, grant writing or even organizing a simple Capitol Hill day to talk about policy or regulatory issues that impacted their community.

Using the same principles of better pricing and more service, the non-profit community helped GSP's growth reach the next order of magnitude and eventually rivaled the technology sector as our second largest group within our client portfolio.

One very good case study of some of the early work in the non-profit community came from one of our first clients, a Pittsburgh-based environmental education organization called RiverQuest (formerly Pittsburgh Voyager). The mission of RiverQuest was born from the need for math, science and environmental education for children from the ages of fifth grade to twelfth grade. A group of concerned parents launched the 501(c)(3) organization and started it with a modest budget.

Soon after its inception RiverQuest received an offer from the U.S. Navy to provide two mothballed Korean War-era PT boats which, if adapted properly, would serve as "floating classrooms" for the students they would host on board. The concept of retrofitting the vessels to simultaneously accommodate two classes of kids and outfitting them with the necessary laboratory equipment to conduct experiments along the three rivers would require funding.

GSP was retained to identify federal and state funding for this effort, and we were successful in securing both. The federal government, through the legislative leadership of Senator Arlen Specter, Senator Rick Santorum and Congressman Mike Doyle, found several U.S. Department of Education grants for RiverQuest in back to back fiscal years, totaling over $350,000. These funds were used for curriculum and programming development.

The Commonwealth of Pennsylvania also released funding to help RiverQuest with money for operations and to expand its footprint to include several new counties in which to operate.

The Final Ingredient — The Band of Merry Men (and Women)

So how were we able to make money by doing more for less?

The final ingredient in the secret sauce was one word — team. Yes, Robin Hood needed his band of merry men and women, and they had to believe in the same business model he did to succeed.

So John and I went out to look for our Friar Tuck, our Little John and our Maid Marian. We needed to assemble the right team and incent them to forego higher salaries for a chance at equity in a growing, hungry consultancy. By asking employees to take less salary with the upside of equity, we could maintain lower overhead costs and foster a business model featuring affordable pricing for clients in a new market.

In our business, most of our competition exists in two forms. First, there are boutique consultancies like GSP that have no more than a handful of principals focusing on sustaining a lifestyle business. Most of these shops average about six to eight employees with a few of these groups growing to a sizeable shop of perhaps twenty employees.

But the prevalent model in our business is the law firm model whereby there is an established in-house lobbying group tucked inside a law firm, usually located in D.C. or in a state capitol. Their lobbyists are employees of the firm and share administrative support, but for the most part are free agents protecting their own client lists and buying hours from one another when they need help on a client.

The differences in the lobbying universe between us and most of our competitors were very stark. GSP's model was much more team-oriented and collegial. In fact, we designed it so that no one person in the firm owned a relationship with a client. Sure, we had account managers that were the day-to-day interface with a client but for the most part, the client would see the benefits of the entire team working on projects for them.

This had two immediate benefits. First, it prevented GSP lobbyists from leaving the firm and clients migrating over with the former employee to their new shop. This is a relationship business and if we had a departing employee, we wanted the client to have the choice of staying with GSP. When one person left a team of five or six, it was easier for the client to believe that the institutional knowledge of their history and effort would remain with GSP while also ameliorating concerns over GSP providing a continuum of service with little to no speed bumps in the absence of the ex-employee. Worst case scenario, GSP would at least have our day in court to avoid client attrition.

Secondly, the clients received the benefit of the combined domain expertise and networks from the team as a whole. Therefore, if the client was visiting the Hill and I had a better relationship with an office or elected official than one of my staff, I would be the lead in that meeting. I cannot stress enough how helpful this was to staying true to our philosophy of granting our clients a higher level of service or "TLC."

So in the end, the early years of GSP were populated by a younger, less celebrity-laden team with humble offices and a honed middle-market strategy. We had a team that would risk salary for ownership and in return, were as hungry as the majority owners. All of this typified the GSP way.

Some of our biggest differences, though, were less about being a disruptive lobbying firm and more about being a different kind of company. A few of these things happened by accident because frankly when we started, we had no idea what was in store for us.

One of the earliest decisions we made was to run GSP as an extremely "flat" organization. There were no titles and no clear hierarchy. When our first employee, Amy Ross (now Kaminski), joined the firm, she was fairly new to the industry. Regardless, we always referred to her and she operated as our "partner," even though she didn't officially own shares of the company yet. The same was true of other new staffers as we brought them on.

Employees like Alyssa Kunselman and Tom Beresynak left jobs from places like Verizon and Dick Corp, now dck worldwide to renew careers at a start-up venture, and in doing so risk job security for a chance to make more and build something better through partial ownership. Staffers like Michelle Schmidt took a chance by leaving one of the country's largest technology councils to join GSP. Jonathan Fasson, a Carnegie Mellon engineering graduate who could have made three or four times what he was making at GSP, instead chose the entrepreneurial route as opposed to the more traditional way.

To the outside world, everyone at GSP looked like equals and, internally, people acted that way.

Now, I know this isn't some kind of groundbreaking idea. Lots of young and innovative businesses have these kinds of informal org charts, no titles, etc. But, unlike most of those other businesses, our rationale was different. We weren't just doing it to be cool or radical. It was all part of a larger plan.

From Day One, John and I were very mindful of what it would take to build a scalable business, which is not common in our industry. We resisted the temptation to name the business after ourselves. While "Kuklis and Associates" has a nice ring, it would not have set us up for the kind of growth or, in John's case, the eventual exit we wanted. When you put your name on the front door, the clients will always want YOU to service their business. With only so many hours in the week, that limits the number of accounts you can effectively represent. Then, if you try to hand off those clients to a so-called "junior" staffer, the client feels as if they are being demoted. That doesn't work.

By positioning everyone in the company as an equal partner, at least in our true start-up years, we could spread that client pressure across lots of people in the organization. Naturally, while I would get involved in highly important accounts or in any account that needed my level of expertise, the expectation of my time and attention was much less onerous. We marketed GSP based on the system and processes we created, not based on the talents of one or two key people. When John moved on to start his new company, we didn't lose a single client as a result. That is very unusual in a personal network and service business like ours and would have been nearly impossible had his name been on the door.

Dance with the One That Brought You

I'll tell you a little secret. It's hard to imagine that anyone was more surprised about our early successes than John and I. With all the widespread skepticism in the market, "Who the hell are we?" became one of our favorite rallying cries. Looking around at our more established competitors, with their star-studded teams of former legislators, their massive political action committees (PACs), and their decadent office buildings, we still had to wonder if we could sustain what we had built.

Sometimes, these waves of self-doubt would cloud the decisions we made. Early on, we assumed that we were successful despite the fact that we were relative nobodies. As time passed, we came to understand that our success might have been because we were nobodies. It forced us to hustle, to work harder, and to be more creative. Unfortunately, it took a few missteps before we figured that out.

As we gained a sliver of prominence and "hipness" in the market, not to mention deeper pockets, GSP became a more attractive destination for a higher caliber employee. We saw this as our first opportunity to bring real "names" into our stable. We fell victim to making hires based on a name or perceived political worth and didn't stay true to the principles that made the company strong – and different.

Despite stellar resumes and deep Rolodexes, a few of these early hires were a colossal failure. Dropping a few perceived "big guns" into a cauldron of scrappy, young, blue collar hustlers was an absolute recipe for disaster. Nobody at GSP had administrative assistants. Everybody booked their own travel and shared hotel rooms when they could. We developed a different corporate culture that tagged along with our different business model and we needed to respect that in the end.

These were the first of many lessons we learned about being true to the vision we had created. Every time we tried to be something we weren't, it backfired. Our clients liked working with us because we were service-oriented and hard-charging. Our employees worked day and night for us because we treated everyone as equals and we stood for something bigger than a bottom line. The political community rooted for us because we were the underdogs. For us, that was enough.

The Entrepreneurial Code

If anything about this book suggests that what we did was easy, then that's a failure in my writing style and not even marginally true. For every success I experienced, there were a dozen failures, polite rejections, or plain-old slaps in the face. A mentor of mine used to say that starting your own business was like "crawling naked through glass." Maybe that's not the most pleasant visual, but it generally captures the essence of it.

I've met three types of people in the entrepreneurial world. First, there are the people who are sufficiently crazy enough to crawl through that glass, often several times over. Then, there are the people who, due to some personal circumstance (maybe a financial hardship or family struggle) could never take the entrepreneurial leap, but admire and root for the people who do. Finally, there are the people who want to step out on their own but lack the courage. These people, I have found, not only resent the people who do take that risk, but even go so far as to sabotage them when they can.

Sadly, in the business of government and politics, there are A LOT of the third type. And, for John and me, the perception among this third type was that we, at our young ages, hadn't paid the "appropriate dues" of spending two decades in bureaucratic purgatory to earn our stripes before setting out to launch GSP Consulting. Thus, the resentment for what we did was even deeper among those people. "Who do they think they are?" wasn't just something whispered behind our backs but was even, on occasion, muttered straight to our faces.

What boosted morale for us in our early days were other entrepreneurs. These business owners celebrated the risk we were taking and went out of their way to work with us because of it. There were friends like John Brabender and Rob Aho of Brabender Cox and Stan Rapp of Greenlee Partners that understood what it was like to be an entrepreneur in a market segment that didn't look fondly at change. These guys had been through the process of starting their own businesses and understood what it took to make it.

When we started GSP, John Brabender offered to provide us with temporary office space in one of his businesses that was experiencing its own downturn. They had recently built out space for nearly 60 employees but with the slip in the economy circa 2001 they were down to a dozen full time employees. But John is one of the most successful political advertisers of our generation and even for an accomplished businessman like himself, he too would experience the ups and downs of the business rollercoaster from time to time.

When we told him we were striking out to start up the company, he quickly offered to house us at no cost. It was then when I started to learn about this unwritten code among entrepreneurs. I didn't understand it then, but I do understand it now.

While we were housed at their office, Brabender arranged for their marketing staff to help us design GSP's branding and marketing materials at cost, and eventually their creative team pulled together the original design of the GSP Consulting logo and our first pieces of collateral material. It's that kinship between fellow entrepreneurs that appeals to and fascinates me even to this day.

Another great friend, Stan Rapp, and his colleagues over at Greenlee Partners, are yet one more example of the unwritten code between entrepreneurs. John and I got to know Stan during our time with Senator Santorum. Stan's company was and is the pinnacle of state government affairs in Pennsylvania, and Stan's longtime friendship with my old boss often pulled me into meetings or casual settings with him, allowing us to start a mutual friendship. Stan recognized the risk John and I were taking by starting GSP and he offered early on in our nascent endeavor to make us "Greenlee Pittsburgh" if the company failed. Some may think this was just lip service but Stan was serious, recognizing in us that same indomitable entrepreneurial spirit he possessed.

During our first few years in business, we often partnered with Greenlee, and eventually when we opened our Philadelphia office in 2003, Stan and his Philadelphia-based partner, John McNichol, allowed us to share office space with them in their Center City facility. When the building management arranged for the name GSP to be affixed on the shingle outside the office front door, we joked about how GSP really stood for "Greenlee's Secret Partners."

To this day we still collaborate with Stan and Greenlee and even though we compete against one another from time to time, I will always be grateful for the opportunity that guys like Stan Rapp and John Brabender bestowed upon us. The lessons I learned from them haven't been lost. As both GSP and now Duane Morris Government Strategies, we have offered similar assistance to other startups as a way of continuing to pay the "code of the entrepreneur" forward.

Go West Young Man

As we looked to grow GSP outside of the Pittsburgh and Pennsylvania markets, we took yet another unconventional approach but one that was consistent with our strategy and brand. The obvious growth tactic would have taken us into large markets like New York, Chicago or Los Angeles. That's how most PR or advertising agencies would expand their footprint.

Most lobbying firms, however, don't expand geographically at all because they brand themselves based on connections and influence they have in a certain geographic footprint like Harrisburg or Columbus. At GSP, we were selling a process and a service model that could theoretically replicate itself in any geographic market.

When we researched new markets for growth, we looked for a set of circumstances that we believed were inherent in our Pittsburgh success. First, we started with what would be considered second-tier markets, where there was an onus on economic development, particularly tech-based economic development. With that, we knew there would be a lot of community and political support for the types of projects and companies we represented. We could align ourselves with technology trade associations and tech-based non-profits, which provided an instant network of contacts and support.

Then, we looked for areas with a strong foundation of research, particularly through major universities and hospital systems. These institutions would provide the farm team of young start-ups we looked to represent as well as the non-profit partners that were often required for government grant and appropriations dollars.

Finally, we looked for markets that were represented in Congress by members of key committees, especially Appropriations. This would ensure that we could tap the necessary political muscle to push things through the legislature and various agencies when we needed it. In Pennsylvania, we had these kinds of resources in the late Congressman John Murtha, a powerhouse on Defense Appropriations and the late Arlen Specter, Chairman of Senate Appropriations Subcommittee for Labor, Health and Human Services and Education.

In the end, we started with places like Tampa, where then Chairman Bill Young controlled many of the Congressional purse strings and directed support to the University of Southern Florida and the Tampa Bay Technology Forum. Then we went to Cleveland, where Congressman Ralph Regula was known for his appropriations prowess and where we could tap into the Cleveland Clinic, Case Western and trade groups and incubators like BioEnterprise and JumpStart for new research and technology. After these, we went to Madison, Wisconsin; the Twin Cities of Minnesota; Ann Arbor, Michigan; and beyond. Some were successful and some weren't. But the overall strategy worked really well for us and allowed us to grow the business much faster than if we had jumped into larger, more saturated markets.

Entrepreneurship & The Importance of Team

Starting a company is brutally hard. Lots of sleepless nights, self-doubt, and the feeling that the whole world is against you could beat almost anyone down. When you get turned down by banks for startup loans because you haven't been in business for two years, or when you are on the phone with credit card companies telling them why their monthly payment was late, it takes a toll on your personal morale. Having a team of true believers standing beside you was incredibly helpful early on, knowing that someone else was in the same foxhole.

When you start your own business, my most important piece of advice is this – burn the boats. The Spanish conquistador Cortez upon arriving in the "new world" ordered his crew to burn their boats. This way the sailors wouldn't be thinking about going home. They had to make it work. Their survival depended on it.

In small business it is much of the same. I think if I could have folded my new company into an existing one or if I had an "out," I may have been tricked into taking it. But when those shadows of self-doubt crept into the recesses of my mind, my team was there for me, as I was for them.

Each member of the "band of merry men" played a different role. Tom Beresnyak was more of the cheerleader, goading me on with dreams of the maiden voyage of "GSP One," the mythical private jet that we would own one day that would allow me to escape the connector flights that never "connected" and left me stranded in many airports around the country. He would also fill my head with ideas of "Joe TV," an ever-looping propaganda reel of GSP successes played in the waiting room of our Station Square offices.

Or Amy Kaminski, ever the opposite of Tom, used reverse psychology to motivate us. She knew that telling us what we couldn't accomplish would light a fire under us, forcing us back up and over that high and distant hill. But we were all in it together, and having the right team meant all the difference in the world.

Six months before we started GSP, I was talking to a handful of my colleagues about starting a firm together. This culminated with a dinner one night at the Grand Concourse Restaurant in Pittsburgh, where John and I sat with three others to discuss our impending leap from our government jobs. Ironically, John and I were much closer with the others around the table than we were with each other. We were targeting the launch of GSP for January 2001.

As January approached, situations changed for some of our potential partners, and our good friend Tony Fratto had a once in a lifetime opportunity to assist in the historic Florida recount vote, which eventually was won by President Bush. That opportunity led to Tony taking a position with then Secretary O'Neill at Treasury and ultimately propelled him to the White House press office. Tony now owns Hamilton Place Strategies in Washington, D.C., where he and his colleagues tend to communication and economic development matters internationally for his clients. Although John and I were unlucky in locking Tony into GSP in 2001, Tony made the right decision for himself and his family, and we could not be happier for him in his success.

Others we had talked to began to drop off as well. Call it cold-feet or whatever you want but the prospects of leaving a stable job and guaranteed salary is frankly too much for most people to handle. Before I knew it, John and I were the last two standing.

"Are you still in?" I remember him asking me.

"You're damn right," I said.

Even though we might not have been the most likely pairing among the group, there we were, the only two people left and crazy enough to go all-in.

Looking back, I'm not sure GSP would have worked if it was anyone other than us. We were so uncannily different, with skills and personalities that complemented one another perfectly.

John was the consummate networker. In fact, he is the best networker I have ever met. I always like to say that you could drop him out of an airplane into a city where he knew no one, and within days he would be sitting behind home plate watching a baseball game with the city's Mayor or most prominent CEOs. He evangelized the business we were building and made believers out of everyone. But John would be the first to admit that government expertise and business management were not his forte.

While John was running around telling the story of GSP and building partnerships, I was hard at work building and managing the company. I was able to build a series of repeatable processes across sales, operations and client service that helped sustain the company and our growth. I also handled the service of our most valued clients. All of the clever branding and marketing would mean nothing if we couldn't actually deliver value for our clients. It was my job to make sure that happened.

I've always had a knack for sales and service, but I also needed to find other employees who could grow professionally into leadership roles in the firm over time. Our hope was that the promise of equity in lieu of higher initial salaries would lure like-minded, entrepreneurial talent in our field to take a leap of faith with us.

Two of those folks were Amy Kaminski and Aaron Grau. I had gotten to know Amy through an internship while working with Senator Santorum. An incredibly diligent and detail-oriented worker, I knew from the onset that I may be able to convince her to leave a position with a large, reputable PR firm to join GSP.

John was not so convinced. He had two other candidates in mind for the same position. I knew John was familiar with Amy and wondered about the cause of his reticence. Over a beer he told me he liked the other candidates more but he was willing to listen to her during an interview. I asked what his concerns were and what it would take to win his support of her candidacy.

In all honesty I don't even remember what the issues were but I intently took notes and when we parted ways, I did something that I needed to do – I emailed Amy the list of concerns that night so she could prepare to answer the questions he had for her the next day. Not exactly fair, but Amy was hired the following week.

Regardless of my "brilliant" intelligence gathering skills, Amy would have won John over in the interview anyway. She had a skillset and talent that we desperately needed and one that would strengthen the foundation of the team. Over the next ten years she proved us right and went on to become one of the pillars of our company as our CFO and COO.

Aaron Grau was a bit of a different story, one more of serendipity. Aaron owned a small lobbying shop in Washington, D.C. and was moving his young family from D.C. to Pittsburgh. Like most Pittsburghers, his wife once told him that with a young family it may be best to move out of D.C. and relocate "home" to a more family-friendly environment. That was code for Pittsburgh as the destination.

Aaron wondered how he could continue his D.C.-based practice from 250 miles away and began sending inquiries out to folks in Pittsburgh. One of his resumes landed on the desk of a mutual friend, Jon Delano. Delano was a former senior staffer for then Congressman Doug Walgren and had moved on from that position ironically because my old boss defeated Mr. Walgren for his seat several years prior. But as most of us political hacks understand, business is business and Jon and I grew our acquaintance from opposite sides of the table into a long-term friendship.

When he received the resume, he passed it along to me, hoping the connection would be mutually beneficial. John, Amy and I interviewed Aaron extensively and in the interview, found the guy who would run our federal shop for the next ten years.

I cite these short examples for fellow entrepreneurs because being in business for yourself is tough. If there is a lesson to be learned it is to make sure you are in business with people you can trust.

Let me illustrate this further. Often for weeks at a time, John and I were two ships passing in the night, seldom seeing each other in the office. But we talked on the phone every night and, over seven years, I can't remember a single time when we had a major disagreement about anything. I trusted him to handle his domain and he trusted me to handle mine, unequivocally.

Most importantly, we were driven by the same sense of purpose and that made it much easier to get through the tough days. If you're ever planning to start your own business, find your own band of merry men and women if you can. It makes a world of difference.

Overall, the world is mostly run by big companies, big interests and big money. Mostly. But, what helps me sleep at night is this – the small, the agile and the idealistic can still win. Big enterprises inevitably lead to lumbering bureaucracies, risk-aversion and complacency, leaving the door open for companies like GSP – or companies like yours – and the dozens of our clients who are creative and driven enough to fight the odds.

To all those Robin Hoods out there who are fighting every day to make a difference and live their dream I say this – we need to find one another and work together. Whether you are a first-term legislator trying to pass groundbreaking legislation, a not-for-profit leader working to raise awareness for an important cause, or a fellow entrepreneur trying to change the world with your new widget, we are all fighting the same fight. True innovation and growth in America will not come from the "good ol' boys' networks." It will come from people like you, who are visionary and courageous enough to put your career and your reputation on the line for something bigger.

While today it is all too easy to look at Washington through a cynical and disillusioned lens, we still have the greatest government in the world. It's a government that can help to foster innovation, serve as a launching pad for a new cause and reach out and give a hand up, not a handout, to the little guy. Know that Washington, for all the misperceptions and faults, remains a valuable resource for all entrepreneurs, and you owe it to yourself to explore its options.

CHAPTER TWO:

The ABCs of Lobbying

How does a company or organization know it needs a lobbyist? Generally, they don't. Typically they have an "Oh no!" moment and are forced into a situation where they need to find someone to handle an issue or help to get them over a particular hurdle. There are also many times when a company simply needs additional capital and turns to a lobbyist for assistance in finding it. However, these "Oh no!" moments are usually discovered in the eleventh hour of the political process and in many respects if identified earlier could have been resolved with less effort in the political or government realms.

GSP and lobbying companies like us are well positioned to help clients identify their specific current and future government needs. However, some clients are naturally better positioned than others to affect the changes necessary to assist them in righting their own ship.

Larger companies with greater resources like trade association support, internal government affairs assistance such as an in-house lobbyist or even a corporate political action committee can quickly and effectively mobilize their cadre of elected officials more so than the average medium-sized organization that may not have these assets in their company's toolkit.

GSP specialized in helping these smaller organizations find their way when government issues presented themselves. For example, one of GSP's first clients was Phipps Conservatory and Botanical Gardens in Pittsburgh, Pennsylvania. The internationally renowned conservatory was in the midst of launching a capital campaign to raise dollars to renovate and expand their facility and in turn, looked to the federal, state and local government entities for support in this endeavor.

Phipps had three phases of renovation and expansion in mind. The first two phases would encompass an over $35 million overhaul and expansion including introducing many new green and clean technologies in the construction. Their Executive Director, Richard Piacentini is a true visionary and traveled the globe looking for new ideas and technologies to introduce into the expanded facility with the concept of showing the developer world that green building could be done.

The third phase of the project is being completed as this book is being printed and consists of the construction of a "living building" which exceeds platinum LEED certification and would be one of the first living buildings east of the Mississippi.

GSP approached Phipps' Board of Directors about assisting in securing public subsidy for the expansion and renovation. Once we were retained, we helped Phipps secure funding from all three levels of government.

Funding types varied from the creation of new education programs designed to interact with regional school districts to historical preservation to the actual brick and mortar construction of the expanded facility. Much of the public funding required a "local match" which means dollars from private sources. This is a way for government to ensure any grants or loans they approve for projects like Phipps leverage private investments as the government rarely, if ever, is the lead investor in a project like Phipps.

The lesson here is that a small- to medium-sized nonprofit like Phipps entering the marketplace in a sophisticated way (and early enough in the process) helped them tap into millions of dollars of public support for their projects. Phipps now stands as one of southwestern Pennsylvania's first day attractions, bringing in tourists and visitors alike to enjoy its botanical wonders and learn how green building principles can be employed in an affordable and responsible way, fulfilling its mission of educating the general public on the environment.

The Right Person For the Job

When you go to court, you take along your lawyer. When you are audited by the IRS, you call your accountant. It stands to reason, then, that if you're interfacing with the government, you hire someone who can help you develop a proven comprehensive strategic plan for working with government. That person is a lobbyist.

In addition to finding necessary funding for projects, lobbyists work in countless other ways for clients. One example is policy. Often, organizations want to set or make a change in policy or, in other cases, there is a need to change the way some aspect of your business or industry is being regulated.

By way of illustration, our company recently represented a national trade association with a particular interest in promoting the use of a certain type of alternative energy. The association wanted to impact a portion of a tax bill that would encourage users of their alternative energy through federal tax credits and incentives. The hope was that, with this subsidy, businesses would use this alternative energy and cover their costs of making the switch from fossil fuel consumption to a cleaner, more renewable energy source. The benefits to the community would be cleaner air, less dependency on foreign oil, and the creation of new jobs in a burgeoning industry.

The work focused on lobbying a certain set of legislators in both Pennsylvania and Ohio as these targeted Members of Congress were on the fence on the bill. The effort included a grassroots campaign to gather letters to the Members in support of the issue, calls from key influencers to the elected officials themselves or senior staff, letters to the editor to local papers in their district to try and move public sentiment in our client's direction, intercepting the Members at local town hall meetings and educating them on the issue, as well as advocating for their position, and finally, the occasional calls to talk shows to raise awareness of the issue and the pending vote.

This is but one example of how lobbying can impact votes directly on issues that are important to your company or industry segment.

From a lobbyist's perspective, our job is to create a unique and comprehensive government strategy for each of our clients and their needs. Sometimes that means helping navigate them through the barriers to entry of selling their products and services to federal or state governments. To others it means offering a Rolodex of contacts to a group interfacing with the government for the first time and not understanding how to do it on their own.

When hiring a lobbyist, choosing one that suits your needs is of utmost importance. If your company feels that the only way to get a job done is to meet with your state's senator, then by all means find a lobbyist who has a link to that senator. Or, if you are a fledgling nonprofit looking for interaction with and recognition from your local officials, hire a lobbyist who can introduce you to the right people to raise awareness about your organization and your issue on a local level.

For the most part, lobbyists help you understand the political lay of the land, avoid land mines on the political battlefield, and direct you to the most efficient solution to your problem. Just as I implied about taking a lawyer to court or an accountant to an audit, lobbyists have the contacts and the domain expertise to get their clients in front of the people who could solve their issue; quickly, efficiently and to their satisfaction.

To DIY or Not to DIY

At its most basic level, lobbying is something that anyone can do. When you vote, you are exercising your First Amendment rights and "lobbying" for the candidate of your choice. If you write a personal check to a political campaign, again, you're lobbying by participating in the political process. Either way, you are working to affect the outcome of a particular political race because you believe in the convictions of that elected official or that body of government.

Elected officials are a little farther up that same food chain. If a lobbyist is not retained by your firm or organization and a person wants his or her Member of Congress to vote one way or the other on a bill, he or she simply picks up the phone and calls that office and expresses his or her opinion on the vote. He or she can also personally visit with members of Congress in real or virtual town hall meetings or drop by the member's district or Capitol Hill office. Lastly, one can send their Member a letter or email expressing their support or concern for their issues. There are myriad reasons for contacting a Member of Congress: you're paying too much tax; you have a problem with the way something is being enforced; you don't like the way something is being handled. Whatever the case, whether you're a company or an individual citizen, you're going to interface with government at some point, on some level, to try to affect change.

However, if you have a bigger problem or issue and the government is at the heart of the matter, you need to find someone who understands the "halls and walls" of Congress or the state and local government equivalents. That's when it may be prudent to retain a lobbyist.

As lobbyists, we've accrued a certain domain expertise over a significant number of years, working with departments, agencies and legislators. We have become experts in our field by understanding the issues that currently exist, the issues that existed in the past, and the issues we're trying to move forward for our clients. It's our job to have our fingers on the pulse of not just the public but the government as a whole.

Reasons to hire a lobbyist vary from client to client but there's usually a need for some combination of solutions to a problem they are experiencing. Sometimes there is a need for "influence peddling," or using strong relationships a lobbyist maintains with certain legislators to influence the outcome of a bill or in some instances administrative action by a department or agency.

In other situations, clients retain lobbying firms in order to borrow the contacts that a lobbying firm has in their network to expand on their traditional or grassroots lobbying effort.

In even more cases, a lobbying firm is retained to help with general networking for purposes of business development or the development of sales opportunities with government agencies and authorities.

As you can see, lobbyists can weigh in for their clients across a spectrum of needs. It is simply an effort to educate and advocate on behalf of your project, your initiative, your issue or problem. Sometimes it's getting action; sometimes it's as unassuming as making yourself or your organization visible to an important legislator or regulator that has oversight on your project or issue. Sometimes it is even as light a touch as to pass along a message to an elected official by saying "Hey, we're a nonprofit in your district. This is the problem we solve and if there is legislation that affects our industry, feel free to give us a call."

Again, this is the kind of relationship you're looking to build. You can do it yourself or hire a firm like ours to help build it for you. Either way, once you've made that connection, you need to maintain that relationship and continually educate and re-educate the elected official as well as their staff.

Of course, there are other times when you need to take an issue further, and at that point it's almost essential to have a lobbyist step in to help. For instance, getting a bill passed into a law, which is in its own right an art and a science, usually requires the intervention of a lobbying professional.

The scientific element of bill creation is basically a how-to guide for following parliamentarian procedures. The art of the procedure comes in when, as a lobbyist, you overlap that by convincing a legislator to champion your bill either by successfully passing it or in some instances stopping it from passing. This can all seem daunting when looking at it from the outside, but working with government isn't nearly as monstrous a task as people imagine; you just need to know what you're doing.

The First Steps of the How To Guide

Lobbying comes in many different forms and serves a myriad of needs. Whether learning to lobby on your own behalf or hiring someone to do it for you, it is essential to understand how the process works, what your own needs are, and how your objectives are best accomplished.

Understanding and navigating federal and state level policy can be complicated to the most experienced of lobbyists, let alone to the novice CEO trying to help his or her own company. Finding public financing for start-up costs, growth, research and development, or capital improvements is difficult and competitive.

As federal and state laws impact more and more of the economy and with more than $1 trillion spent by the federal government alone each year for goods and services, companies and organizations cannot afford to ignore these concerns and opportunities.

Retaining the services of a lobbying shop will help you engage government more effectively. If you are planning on going down the DIY road, here are some helpful hints to keep you on track:

- First, figure out where your bill is in the parliamentarian process. This is accomplished through a variety of bill tracking sites, the most popular among them being thomas.loc.gov.

The THOMAS website, named after Thomas Jefferson, allows you to track federal bills, administrative actions, Supreme Court activity, download session and committee calendars and respond directly to legislators.

Most state websites have tracking capabilities as well and will serve to track bills in a similar manner for you.

- Second, identify which legislators are primary sponsors or co-sponsors of your bill. Primary sponsors usually introduce the bill and will be expected by their party leadership to rally support for the eventual passage of the bill. The names of these primary sponsors are usually first on the bill, with co-sponsors being listed in alphabetical order thereafter.

Co-sponsors are folks that lend their names to the bill in support of its passage and will be counted on to rally other Members of Congress or their state legislature to vote for the bill.

Primary sponsors and Co-sponsors play a pivotal role in the fate of legislation, so make sure they are your first-tier targets when you begin your personal lobbying effort.

- Look for the "sister" bill. When one chamber of the House or Senate introduces a bill, there is usually a twin bill, or "sister" bill, introduced in the other chamber by sympathetic supporters. If your bill is introduced in the House and has no twin in the Senate, usually this is cause for concern.

A bill can pass unanimously in one chamber and may never advance beyond that stage unless both chambers are in support of the initiative. If your bill is in that awkward place, then work with the sponsoring legislators in the chamber that has the bill to help you identify supporters in the other chamber to advance your cause. Usually if a legislator wants to be a primary sponsor or co-sponsor of a bill, they want to push for passage and will volunteer to help.

- Don't forget about the veto. You can be successful in both chambers of the federal or state legislature and the bill can still be stopped by the Governor or the President. The Executive Branch holds the power to veto the passage of bills, forcing, in many cases, the legislative process to start all over again. When veto power is exercised, it requires a ⅔rd majority override in both the House and Senate. This is no easy task, so ensure that you've not ignored the Governor's Mansion or the White House in your lobbying strategy.

During the mid '90s, I was part of Senator Santorum's appropriations team, working to earmark federal funding for projects of import to Pennsylvania. As part of our work, the Senator wanted to appropriate over $20 million in Defense Military Construction (or MILCON) money to relocate an Army regional headquarters. The Army had a requirement for the expansion and the new location but didn't have the funding with which to build it. The Senator stepped in to champion this effort.

After a year of working to ensure funding was contained in the Senate version of the appropriations bill and identifying similar champions in the House bill, the conference report was sent to then President Clinton to sign.

As fate would have it, earlier in the session, Congress had passed the line item veto power, allowing the President to "redline" parts of spending bills that he or she deemed inappropriate or unnecessary. The Clinton Administration chose to line item veto our project (among others) and the process had to begin all over again.

Luckily in the following year, the Supreme Court ruled that the line item veto was unconstitutional and therefore we were able to ensure the project survived in the subsequent year's MILCON budget. However, we lost a year between appropriations cycles because of veto power. That said, I could say I was the first and only kid on my block ever to have a project line item vetoed. It's not fun but the story has become a tall tale in Kuklis family lore.

Even though the line item veto was deemed unconstitutional at the federal level, some states (and consequently some Governors) do have the ability to redline their budgets in a similar way. Be aware of this power and do not ignore the Governor's Mansion when executing on your legislative strategies.

- Watch the clock. Legislative sessions are tricky, even for the most astute lobbyist. When bills are not passed by the end of a session, they need to be reintroduced and return to the starting gate. This means you may have your bill passed in one chamber and almost passed in another, and you may have to start all over again.

Also, federal fiscal years are different than most state fiscal years. If you are tracking budget and spending bills, "mind the gap" between the two.

- Last, coordinate efforts with like-minded groups. Work with your trade association as much as you can and force them to prioritize the legislation that is important to you. They also retain lobbyists, and sometimes you can piggyback off of their representation to the benefit of your effort.

If there are other companies or organizations that are supportive of your bill, make sure they are weighing in too. You can never have too much support. The more, the merrier!

CHAPTER THREE:

The Chess Board

Although a bit cliché, being successful in lobbying reminds me of playing a competitive game of chess. If you are playing against a neophyte, the game is not very competitive. Usually the more experienced chess player can trick a novice into quick checkmates. When equally matched, that's when the chess board becomes interesting. These lessons easily translate into real life lobbying efforts, whether you are doing your own lobbying or whether you have retained a firm to lead you into battle.

Each chess player starts a game with a strategy based on what it will take to win, understanding how your competitor plays, where their strengths and weaknesses are on the board, and what likely moves will lead to victory.

The variable that differs from theory to practice is at the heart of the game of lobbying, as you may be playing more than one chess game at a time. Consider this – your organization may be looking at multiple efforts in D.C. and your state capitol concurrently. You may have a policy need in D.C. and a contract issue in Columbus. This is where the value proposition of retaining a lobbying firm will pay dividends.

If you are new to the government chess board, let me offer a few thoughts to help guide you in your approach and decision making to this game.

The Game — The Sway of Influence

There are a variety to ways to influence legislators and elected officials. Legislators are not influenced by the business-oriented. It doesn't matter to them if they are generating wealth for your company; after all, that's your job. Simply put, what influences a legislator is answering the following question — what community or economic good will this action serve? And to the less civic-minded in my industry, will this action help him or her get reelected?

Juxtapose the thought process and realize that an argument or pitch that might work for an investor of your company needs to be worded differently when you are presenting it to a legislator. Telling a legislator, "Invest in this and it's going to create $8 for each $1 that you invest," isn't going to matter. Instead, legislators care if you're going to create new jobs, save lives, or improve the community by knocking down a dilapidated building and putting up a new one that will generate tax revenue.

Sometimes the messages a lobbyist crafts in order to influence legislators are somewhat generic. Lobbyists use enticements to which every legislator is sure to react. In other instances they are very specific or targeted to different views. For one legislator, a lobbyist may take a more green, or community-oriented approach to their argument, and with the same client offer a different argument to a legislator that is more motivated by discussing the business or tax base aspects of the project. It's simply crafting the message to influence the specific audience you are visiting that moment.

In the end, a good project hits on many points that, regardless of political party or philosophical bend, will encourage a civic-minded elected official to act on behalf of clients, and as you can see, there are a variety of ways my industry handles that sway of influence.

The Chess Pieces

On every chess board stands two armies facing one another with the exact same pieces at the beginning of each game. Players have important pieces like kings and queens, all the way down to a row of pawns that constitute your army. Each piece moves in its own way, possessing different abilities, and thus, each piece is valued differently.

This is not true of the playing board in the game of lobbying. Not every client has the same resources, political or economic gravity, experience or budget. Every client is playing a unique game unto themselves, and it is our job to ensure they maximize the pieces they have on their respective chess boards.

Many outside of our realm feel that money influences the outcome of all political events. I won't lie – it has a major impact. However, sometimes knowing when and how to attack with the smallest of pieces render the most powerful pieces on the chess board impotent.

Remember, you and your organization are the "king" on the chess board. Your entire government strategy depends upon you protecting the king and capturing the king from the opposition. The following sections will outline the chess pieces of lobbying and give you a better sense how to use them.

The Rolodex (or Queen)

Contacts are the lifeblood of my business. There are two sides to this business: One side possesses and maintains the domain expertise of what we do. People who have worked in various departments or agencies in D.C. or state capitols, who know how to get projects funded with grants or contracts because they've done it before.

Then, there's the Rolodex. If I can't get a meeting for one of my clients, I lose the client. Maintaining and growing your personal political Rolodex and the political Rolodex of your company or organization remains critical to your chance of success.

Understanding when to use this network is almost as important as having it. For example, your organization may have a need to get the Governor's attention on a matter. If that's the case, what is the best way in which to do this? At a political fundraiser? In the papers with a letter to the editor? Calling the local office of the Governor and demanding an audience?

If you are a DIY lobbyist, you must be able to gauge the level of need and decide where to spend your "political capital." Sometimes that five minutes on the phone with the Governor is worth 10 years of work because it solved a major problem for your company. Use it wisely.

But you need to be careful to not overspend your political cache or risk putting your queen in a dangerous position on the board. If you go to the Governor one too many times, you become *persona non grata*. You never want someone to say, "Oh no, not you again." If you're parsimonious in your requests as a lobbyist and careful about when and how you expend your political capital, you will remain in favor with the elected officials with whom you work, and your clients will be well served. It's experience and instinct that teach you those things, and it's this balance that is at the heart of lobbying.

Working With Government – The Domain Experts (or Rooks)

Navigating the government marketplace takes connections, networking skills, and a certain level of finesse. The halls of government can be tedious and time-consuming to the average CEO or director of a non-profit organization. Successful legislative strategies are based on having a seat at the table when decisions are being debated and maintaining relationships with the players at that table so they can help you when it is time for a vote or approval.

There's value in retaining a group like ours to help you in your initial foray into the government process. Being well-acquainted with the ins and outs of government has definite benefits. The federal government can be seen as one gigantic marketplace – you simply cannot find a bigger customer. The government will buy products and services you are looking to sell. It is also a great philanthropic engine that – among other things – funds grants that no one else would fund, and conducts research that no one else wants to support financially. The government realizes that it's getting a community or economic benefit from its efforts, so they continue to budget accordingly.

Focusing on government contracting or, in our language, procurement, establishes a primary and secondary marketplace for selling your products and services. Government checks don't bounce, and they buy everything from paper clips to Stealth Fighters. Understanding how to maximize your chances of success in the marketplace can really enhance the bottom line and sales funnel for a sophisticated company.

Governments at the federal, state and local levels all possess different purchasing practices but maintain similar protocols for working with companies of all shapes and sizes. Usually government agencies have a centralized vendor registration system that require certification of your company before you can offer any products or services to them. This is usually an administrative process which, depending on the level of government, can take a few clicks on a keyboard or put you on a yearlong waiting list.

At the federal level, the General Services Administration (GSA) is the clearinghouse for this activity. The GSA requires a process for certification in many cases for their vendors called the GSA Schedule. Each market segment has its own schedule, and if you are interested in doing business with the federal government you first need to make sure you have secured approval on the correct and relevant schedule that fits your company and its services.

Some lobbying and consulting firms have internal domain experts that can help expedite the GSA scheduling process as in some cases can average a year from start of the process to final approval. Having an expert that has completed GSA scheduling for their clients may be worth the fee to accomplish this.

Once on the schedule, your company will receive RFP notifications from federal departments and agencies that may be of interest to you. It is important, however, to make sure you have an understanding of the government buying practices and compliance protocols before trying to navigate this complex process on your own.

It should be recognized, however, that government knows that it is not in its best interest to be detrimental to business. We've all heard horror stories about red tape, taking forever to get paid, or money that came with so many strings attached it's almost like not getting any money at all. Don't get me wrong, sometimes those negative experiences are true, but because of their subject matter expertise or connections, saying yes to lobbyists can only help your experience be a positive one. Among other things, lobbyists can cut through red tape or influence the outcome of an effort, whether it's for money, policy, regulatory affairs, or something else entirely.

Second, a strong understanding of government buying practices and compliance protocols will help you as you approach the government as a customer. Again, various practices differ at the federal, state and local level for procurement practices but the themes are the same. Once you have established your certification as a vendor, the next step will be to identify business that you can win.

In some instances, your company may possess a new technology, product or service that the government has yet to test or measure. Your marketing effort then will require a targeted business development strategy to choice agencies that fit your product segment.

In order to do this effectively, you won't be able to sit back and let RFPs come to you. You will have to do some door knocking at the right agencies to generate interest from the related program officers that would like to test or buy your new product. But first they need to know you and your product are out there.

So how do you find the right contacts?

There are websites, some free and some in which you will need to subscribe, that allow you to identify the right contacts at federal and state agencies. The most popular free site is called "FedBizOpps." This site allows you to register your company to receive information about relevant contract opportunities and track current government contracts that might be attractive to you. Other pay sites out there may offer more information, but a good sales person knows not to wait for reactive information but to be proactive in their intelligence gathering. If you can afford the pay sites, they usually pay dividends and put you ahead of the curve.

However, sometimes these subscriptions and tracking mechanisms aren't enough. You may have identified a likely contract worthy of pursuit but you cannot make the right contact at the agency to learn more.

Here's a trick of the trade – contact your legislator and ask their office for assistance. Keep in mind that these elected officials are your advocates. They want to bring government business to a constituent company and they have constituent service staffers that can help you learn how to track and attack these opportunities. Don't expect them to be available to you like a paid employee, but they have a few ways they can help in your strategy to meet the right contacts.

First, each legislator, whether they are federal or state-related, has a hotline into all federal or state agencies. At the end of this hotline is a public official known as a legislative liaison. These liaisons are responsible in part for answering congressional inquiries. They can, if asked, help with constituent matters on behalf of the elected official.

The tactic here is to convince your representative or their staffer that you have a product or service worth selling to the government and that you need a proper introduction made to the right procurement officer within your target market. The office will likely need to make a call to the department or agency through their liaison to determine who that is and, once identified, can help you arrange a meeting.

Don't abuse this relationship. Make sure only to tap into this when appropriate. Develop your own relationship with the procurement folks inside the agency, but if you cannot find your way in, this may help expedite the process for you.

Secondly, if you have contacts with the potential buyers now, it is a matter of understanding what contract opportunities may be available and how can you position yourself to compete to win. Pursuing government contracts is highly competitive. To be successful, you need to have timely information granting you the most time to respond to an opportunity and create quality relationships with those who will buy your products and services. Getting to know your program managers and acquisition officers is a good first step, but it is only that – a first step.

You will need to focus on a number of steps to be successful:

- Step one in this process is identifying any potential requirements that you as the vendor can fill. Government agencies will publish their required procurement needs anywhere from six months to three years out as they prepare their budgets. Pay attention to these requirements as they will help you sniff out the real opportunities.

- Step two is the identification of funding mechanisms. Just because the government agency has a requirement to purchase a product doesn't always mean it has the funding to buy. I know, this concept is counterintuitive but sometimes various departments will have a requirement for an order but will be over budget or worst case, not have the budget to purchase the good or service at all. You will need to track the budgets as well as the requirements to make sure you are chasing a contract that can actually be fulfilled.

You may recall a few years back when Senator John Kerry, the Democratic presidential hopeful, came under media scrutiny for his votes on bulletproof vests for our troops in Afghanistan and Iraq. The military had a requirement for the protective vests but did not have any money to purchase additional equipment. Emergency measures were taken in Congress to vote to appropriate additional funds for the war effort. This is just one example of a government entity, in this case the U.S. Department of Defense, having a requirement to provide gear but not maintaining the budget to acquire it.

- The third and final step in your effort will require you to identify the influences that can be brought to bear to determine the outcome of any contract you seek. These influences can be both internal and external.

Internal influences often relate to matters of regulatory restrictions (such as the need to purchase items that require an agency approval to use for safety, etc.), programmatic guidelines (such as the need to purchase products that may be made by adhering to "green and clean" principles) or finally cyclical constraints (budget season).

External influences relate to items such as political influence (a contract may be influenced by legislators on the right committee fighting for work in their home districts or for a constituent company) or current events (such as war, terrorist attacks, natural disasters, health epidemics, etc.).

Set-Aside Work

The government at all levels has an interest in promoting a variety of special category businesses and their growth. Some examples are promoting small business, contracts for women and minority owned businesses, helping businesses located in distressed or blighted communities, or even helping businesses owned by the service disabled veteran community. Oftentimes government agencies set aside a portion of their contracts for businesses to promote economic development in these aforementioned areas.

If you believe your business may qualify for one or more of these special designations, it will undoubtedly help you secure government work. Many federal and state agencies have requirements to contract with companies that fit into these categories as do many of the large contract integrators that the government employs on big contracts.

These contract integrators are private companies but have won a consulting contract with the government to build a tank or some other project that will require multiple vendors and suppliers to complete. Many of their contracts will require them to subcontract work to disadvantaged businesses as part of the contract requirements.

In order to qualify as one of these vendors, contact the procurement officers at your targeted agencies to learn how to certify yourself. There is a federal designation and in many cases, separate state and local designations to accomplish this. Some designations automatically reciprocate for other levels of government and in other cases, you need to qualify separately.

This process can be as simple as a few page application at a local government office to a several month process requiring financials, budgets, proof of ownership, etc., at the higher levels of government. Again, if you are uncertain or do not have the in-house capacity to handle this, groups like ours exist and can be retained to help you through these processes.

Economics and Government

When it comes to contracting with government entities, the overwhelming notion is that the government is cheap, and that a bid for a contract will always go to the lowest bidder. That changed years ago, and the government now exercises a "best value" proposition. Best value means you don't always have to be low bidder to win a competitive contract process. Government procurement officers these days can account for past performance on similar contracts and decide that, although your company may have the third lowest bid, you have provided excellent work in the past and can choose you over companies that may come in at a lower price point but didn't score as high on past performance.

Both federal and state governments offer sole-source contracts where there is no bidding war but instead, based on the dollar threshold of the contract and past performance of the firm, the department or agency reserves the right to award the contract with no bidding process to an approved or scheduled vendor. The dollar thresholds for these types of contracts vary but are usually small. At the state level these thresholds ballpark on average around $100,000 to $200,000. At the federal level, small is a relative term. Some federal sole-source thresholds are as "low" as $3,000,000.

There are many instances in which a company, not for wanting, doesn't know the stiff competition its up against. In order to simply level the playing field a bit, we can help sniff out who the competition is and why they tend to win. Firms like ours are often paid to help with items such as:

- Client readiness evaluations (are you ready to chase a government contract and if not, what do you need to do to get ready?);
- Contract opportunities evaluation;
- Meeting with agency representatives and assisting in the interpretation of those interfaces (what did they mean versus what did they say);
- And of course, contract negotiations.

Again, it's all about contacts converging with domain expertise to create and environment to capture the sales opportunity.

One final thought on government sales - companies are often asked to commit as part of the contracting process to offer the government "best price," which means you have to give the government the same price for your product or service as you would your best customer. In layman's terms, you will have to provide the government with fair market value on your product. Expect this going into the process as we remember the horror stories in the 1980s with $80 hammers and $500 toilet seats bought by the Pentagon. Those days are long gone.

All government purchases, save for some military top-secret buys, are available publicly and no good bureaucrat wants to raise suspicions of watchdog groups or investigative reporters. Be prepared to play fair.

The basic premise is that working with government is difficult, and the idea that an outsider looking to get into the game needs to tiptoe around is simply unfounded. Some of the most successful companies around have government contracts, and there are literally thousands of different types of companies and organizations working with government in ways you might not imagine. What I can't stress enough, however, is the value of a solid internal understanding of how it all works as well as having the right connections in order to make that understanding work to your advantage.

Creating Buzz

Grassroots and Grass Tops (or the Knights and Pawns)

Sometimes making noise about your cause is almost as worthwhile as your cause. If buzz is what you need, then grassroots lobbying is often the fastest way to get the job done.

Grassroots lobbying relies upon a network of broad-ranging relationships within a targeted community to achieve a desired outcome. Sometimes it is educating voters on a referendum ballot question. Other times it is fighting the NIMBY (or "not in my back yard") fight against a chemical plant or prison that may locate in your community.

Grassroots and grass tops lobbying holds a place in many

advocacy campaigns and engaging in grassroots lobbying is an asset in the seasoned lobbyists' tool box.

Grassroots lobbying is effective and focuses on mobilizing support in the community for your project, unlike the traditional lobbying of legislators whereby your group engages the elected official directly. Instead, the concept here is that legislators hear from key influencers in their district or state that have been energized by you or on behalf of your cause. Coupling this grassroots effort with a traditional lobbying effort reinforces your message and ultimately helps you accomplish your goals.

Advocacy for your effort grows from the constituency of communities – the very roots – where passion and energy are found to be the most personal and relevant. When this passion and energy is concentrated effectively to influence the appropriate audience, the end result is success.

When done effectively, your organization should design and implement an effective grassroots and grass tops strategy by identifying and understanding your target audience and then mapping the most effective way to reach that group. First, you will need a better understanding of the grassroots process.

To begin, allow me to define the difference between grass tops and grassroots. A grass top contact is a key influencer in a certain community. They are folks like the chairman of the board of a chamber of commerce, a political party or committee vice chair, a CEO in the community or even a president of a trade association. They are at the "top" of their groups and can influence the "grassroots" beneath them in their respective flowcharts.

“Grassroots” are the rank and file that take direction from the grass tops but can be as effective in many cases. Traditional grassrooters are folks such as a local union member who’s willing to write a letter to their Congresswoman or a local Republican Committeeman that will put a sign in his yard or pen a letter to the editor about your issue. Grassroots usually follow the lead from their grass tops but sometimes can break ranks if the right cause is presented.

Now that you have a better idea of what grassroots lobbying is and differences between grass tops and grassroots, let’s focus for a second on how to lead an effective grassroots campaign and the steps you should take to organize your effort:

- First, you need to create an effective message for your campaign that will resonate with not only your targets among elected officials, but also the grassrooters that you want to mobilize. Usually you and your group can cannibalize the message you are delivering through traditional lobbying means and repurpose it for your grassroots effort.

For example, say you want to sway the vote of a local councilman on a vote to allow a large, big-box chain into your community. Different messages will resonate differently with various members of the community. The chamber of commerce members will react differently than perhaps the environmentalist or the local mom and pop store owners. Your message needs to be tweaked enough to convince each group to rally to your cause regardless of their respective differences between one another.

As both GSP and DMGS, we have worked this exact effort for our clients. A few years back, we were retained by a group of loosely-affiliated business interests who wanted to fight a big-box chain from coming to their town. The neighborhood and all the independent retailers were up in arms about the possible development. We were specifically brought on board to do some grassroots lobbying promoting the idea that this big-box store's arrival would hurt the local independent business owners, possibly causing the small main street stores to close and in doing so, negatively impact the community as a whole. In short, we needed to drum up support in opposition of the development.

In order to garner that support, we set to work finding people to attend rallies; collected signatures on petitions; went to the local papers and got op-ed pieces written about the potential damage that could befall the community and many of its mom and pop store owners; used social media to spread the word; scooped in the not-in-my-backyard folks by dropping fliers door-to-door.

We won.

We kept the development from moving in to the community and the residents and business owners were happy.

In truth, it may not be as sexy as some of the work we do on a day-to-day basis, but it's probably equally as important because it supports a wider swath of community. If you're a small business you need to know that a quality grassroots lobbying campaign can be one of your best friends during a crisis like this.

- The second step consists of identifying the methodology of your grassroots campaign. I've already mentioned a few ways to do this: letters to the editor, op-ed pieces in the local papers, blogging and social media, calls to talk shows to generate buzz, and the like. Not all methods are applicable to each campaign. Find out what will work best for you and for your individual campaigns and implement it.

- Let me illustrate my point. Some campaigns need to be very public. Others can be done with more stealth. There are times when a key influencer can make a call to a target legislator and based on that person's relationship with that elected official convince them to vote one way or the other. There are no rallies, no protests – just the right person picking up the phone or pinging a legislator with an email on behalf of your cause.

- The third step is execution. Now it is time to launch your grassroots campaign. You have your message and methodology, and execution involves several fundamental steps.

My old boss, Senator Rick Santorum likened this part of the effort to a football game by calling it his "ground game." He was an expert at it. After all, few candidates that I am aware of can claim to run a grassroots campaign as effectively and with more alacrity than Rick. Here's a guy that first beat a 14-year incumbent in 1990 even though his opponent outspent Rick three to one. In 1992 the Democratic Governor in Pennsylvania and the Democratic-controlled state legislature tried to gerrymander Rick out of his district by redrawing the districts to be over 70 percent Democrat. Rick won re-election in 1992 despite this political effort winning 63 percent of the vote.

It was under his tutelage that I learned the value of a strong grassroots campaign. During his 1994 race for the U.S. Senate, Rick assembled a regional ground game that included an effort to attract conservative democrats in Allegheny County to cross over and vote for him, as his opponent was a fairly liberal Democrat that did not necessarily identify with the population. Most of western Pennsylvania is populated by Reagan Democrats – blue collar, pro-life, pro-gun catholic Democrats that identified more with Santorum's resume than they did his opponent.

We were tasked with door knocking during the last six weeks of the campaign, hand delivering over 250,000 pieces of targeted literature to likely democratic voters. I was in charge of assembling part of this effort and had to find the right team that would help us with this Herculean effort.

Thankfully, Rick attracted some of the strongest grassrooters with whom I have had the pleasure of working during my time in politics. I had tireless door knockers like Tim Haas and Jeff Iseman who had no fear of knocking some of the tougher neighborhoods in the city of Pittsburgh. Tim was a veteran and believed strongly in Rick's passion to help the Armed Services and Pennsylvania's deep veteran population, while Jeff's passion was grounded in faith and the pro-life community. I even had a 14-year-old kid named Mike DeVanney who spent his weekends delivering literature into parts of the city that were 10 to one Democrat to Republican.

These guys would spend their time with me hanging yard signs and working polling locations on election day, from 7 a.m. to 8 p.m. This is the definition of grassroots. I even had some grass tops guys like Herb Ohliger and Kim Stolfer from the pro-gun communities deliver over 30,000 pieces of literature by themselves in six weeks to a community that helped Rick win the election in 1994 by less than a few percentage points. Without grassroots, we could have lost.

To have an effective ground game, one must understand that grassroots campaigns are volunteer driven. These are the folks who will be willing to take a day off from work to attend a rally or will lend their name to a letter to the editor campaign to advance your issue. But they will need your leadership and help in organizing the effort. Be prepared to send examples of what you want a letter to the editor to look like and let them edit it so that they are comfortable with sending the final version. Be ready to send your volunteers a short script with message points you want them to make when they call the Mayor's chief of staff on your behalf. Anything that makes their effort easier will enhance your chances of them following through.

To that end, also ask for some kind of proof that the volunteer did what they said they were going to do. This is easier than it sounds as you can ask them to blind copy you on the email they send or provide you with a copy of a letter they mailed on your behalf. Some efforts will require trust such as intercepting a legislator at a town hall meeting, but at a minimum ask them how the legislator responded, did staff promise a written response, did others ask similar questions or follow ups, etc. Sometimes this is hard to do as you don't want to appear as if you don't trust the volunteer but, as President Reagan once said of the Soviet arms reduction treaties, "trust but verify."

Your grassroots effort should also include an appreciable amount of media monitoring. Creating that buzz about your issue is often fought through earned media. Earned media is exactly as it sounds – it is earned, not bought. Television commercials, radio spots and banner ads on websites are paid media. Earned media consists of wins, such as getting letters to the editor printed; relevant bloggers blogging about your issue; Facebook users "liking" your cause; or people mentioning your effort on calls to talk shows, during spontaneous media interviews, at a rally or during a protest.

You and your organization should spend some time setting up Google alerts and similar media tracking protocols for keywords related to you or your campaign to ensure you don't miss any earned media coverage, good or bad. This will allow you to respond in a timely manner to Internet media as well as the daily and weekly newspaper outlets.

Also keep a "press watch" or an electronic media clippings file related to your endeavor. This is important as many times you will be required to refer to quotes in previously run articles or related press hits.

Lastly, it is important that you identify the proper surrogates to speak on behalf of your issue. Let's face it, someone that will be willing to help you may be full of passion about your issue but in the end, may not be the right person to be speaking publicly about your topic. A good portion of remarks offered publicly often come "off the cuff," and you want your surrogates to be knowledgeable about your issue or campaign.

Proper surrogates are mostly discovered from the grass tops side of this endeavor, but on occasion you will find a quality grassrooter who can do the job. Grass toppers are usually professionals in their field and are better suited to be offering remarks at a town hall meeting or during a public roundtable discussion with a legislator. Again, it is worth noting that scripting your surrogates with your message will only create better results for your earned media opportunities.

The Government and Grants (or, the Bishops)

Money for Nothing, Almost

To many regular folks, the government seems broke, especially in these challenging economic times. It would seem, then, that finding money for projects and initiatives might not be possible in this day and age and yet, almost daily, we hear of new funding being made available for say, a bridge retrofit or major company expansion. So, where does all the money come from to continually fund projects like this? Congress.

On an annual basis, Congress passes a budget. If you cast yourself back to your ninth grade civics class you may recall that the doctrine of Separation of Powers that polices the three branches of the U.S. government gives the "power of the purse" to Congress.

This process can be complex in practice but in theory it is fairly simple. The federal fiscal year begins on October 1 of every year and Congress settles on a budget during various parliamentarian processes throughout the calendar year. During this annual appropriations cycle, they work to spend the money they have budgeted through a series of spending bills. Anticipated tax revenue is a fairly accurate predictor of how much money they have to spend and how much they need to borrow in order to accomplish what they want to do. Sometimes, our government goes into financial markets and borrows from places like China or institutional lenders in other nations to obtain the money needed in order to run the programs they want to run.

In addition to the federal budget, each state has a budget to which they are required to adhere. Many states are, in fact, constitutionally bound to pass a balanced budget. Sometimes states will end up with a revenue surplus, which can be put into a rainy day fund or expended on services or programs in the current fiscal year. Other times that's a tip-off that a state is collecting to excess through taxes, which allows them to cut back or lower taxes for their citizens.

Whatever the case may be, the vast majority of the budget comes from the taxpayer, and is already earmarked in the budget. If it's not readily available, Congress can add money for particular projects, or line items that need to be increased. If revenue is down, often cuts need to be made and this is when it's imperative that your issues and projects are protected. Retaining a lobbyist like me can pay off by defending funding that is important to you.

As you see, lobbying functions offensively and defensively depending upon client needs. My goal is to represent and defend my clients, and while I personally might have different views than them, I get paid to represent their interests. Basically, I am paid to win. If the interests of my clients get cut, then sometimes I get cut from the picture as well.

However, even though the perception that government budgets may be austere at times, the federal government alone offers thousands of grants on an annual basis that you and your organization may be interested in chasing.

Grants, much like government contracts, are offered through a series of protocols that can be tracked very effectively if you know where to look. Some lobbying groups maintain a subject matter expertise in grant identification and grant writing. GSP and now DMGS offers this service to our clients as do some of our competitors in D.C. and in various state capitols.

Many types of government grants are non-dilutive in nature, meaning your company will not be required to sacrifice equity in return for the funding you will receive. If you are a venture-backed company, your investors will like this aspect.

Coupled with the fact that receiving a grant from a federal or state department or agency often validates your technology or service, this may actually help you pitch new investors as you can say that a government entity believes strongly enough in your product that they have provided public funding to advance your technology or solve a problem that they have. Being able to flag the Department of Defense, Transportation or Energy on your standard investor PowerPoint deck can't hurt when pitching for new money.

There are four steps to successfully securing a grant from any level of government:

- Step one is grant monitoring and identification. The federal government has several free websites that you can subscribe to, the most popular being grants.gov,

Your company or organization can self-certify on grants.gov and in doing so, you will receive notices of funding availability based on grant names, subject name or keyword searches that you wish to identify. For example, let's say your technology company has an interest in any new grant related to traumatic brain injuries. You can track grants related to education, labor or health for TBI. Similar grant sites can also be identified for individual state grants on a state-by-state basis.

- Once you have identified a grant that you think may fit your organization, the next step is grant development. Grant development is the most amorphous of the four grant phases, but can be the most important.

Grant development covers a host of topics important to writing a successful grant. This is the period when, after identifying a grant, your organization is going to make a "go" or "no go" decision on spending an appreciable amount of time in writing a grant. And we all know time is money.

The first step in the grant development process is vetting the grant to identify what it will take to win the grant. Most grant opportunities are not 100 percent fits for your organization out of the gate. You may be required to work with a government entity for example, as part of the eligibility requirement. Or you may be asked to have an economic impact analysis completed and submitted to help the government entity grade your final submission. It is important that during this phase that you are honest with yourself about whether or not this grant is worth pursuing.

Gather all pertinent project information including project details, data information required for the final grant application and other project narratives you can get from past applicants. Remember, through the Freedom of Information Act (FOIA), you can request copies of past grant applications to review past winners and perhaps just as importantly, identify what past losers did so that you can avoid similar pitfalls. Normally grant program managers will offer winners and losers a debriefing that may include a scoring sheet explaining why they were or were not funded. Securing this information can help you decide whether this grant is for you or not.

Grant development also means building relationships with grantors, strategically networking with federal, state and local funding entities. Once a grant is announced publicly, usually you are unable to contact these program managers directly. It is important to develop those relationships before a grant is released so that you can determine what the program managers are looking for in the coming grant round. You don't want to be wasting time if the PM is not going to be funding grants that are related to your work or organization in the coming round.

By way of example, we once saved a Pittsburgh-based client nearly $24,000 in grant writing fees by doing just this. There was a Pennsylvania-based grant that was made available to PA non-profit organizations which included eight different eligible uses. One of those uses included a critical infrastructure component in which our client had a strong interest.

Upon making a call to the Pennsylvania Department of Community & Economic Development (the department through which the grant was being funded and administered) we discovered by discussing with the grant program manager that the state only intended on funding projects in one of the eight areas of eligibility in the coming round. So even though on paper our client's activity was fundable, they would have wasted their time in pursuit of funding in the coming round.

GSP lost some fees for what could have been a nice-sized project, but our client was eternally grateful for saving them not only our fees but the cost of their time in writing a grant they couldn't win.

Grant development is also the stage of the grant process where building strategic partnerships and networking can make or break your final application. If you do identify the need for partners in the community such as a co-applicant or partner, this is where you will need to find organizations willing to commit to the effort.

In the mid 2000s, GSP represented a group of biotech and life science companies in western Pennsylvania. The U.S. Department of Labor had recently released a notice of funding availability for a new grant which would retrain or "up-skill" traditional manufacturing workers with math and science education so that they could get jobs with high tech manufacturers like our clients.

Individually our clients knew that they could apply for their grant but if they pulled their resources together with one another and some local non-profit organizations that they would have a better chance of winning. So, part of our grant development strategy required us to reach out into the regional community to find the right partners to increase our chances of success.

The first step was to identify the organizations that would help with the retraining and up-skilling that the U.S .Department of Labor wanted to see. We found willing partners in both the Community College of Allegheny County (CCAC) and the University of Pittsburgh (Pitt). Both CCAC and Pitt could create or modify current curriculum and classes to accommodate the new programs and with their willingness to partner, they would receive funds from the grant to pay for the retraining.

Secondly, we knew that our clients individually stood a better chance of succeeding if we identified an umbrella primary applicant such as a trade association. This primary applicant was another non-profit organization called the Pittsburgh Life Sciences Greenhouse (PLSG). The PLSG was an organization created several years earlier with both public funds from the state of Pennsylvania and also private sources to help foster the growth of biotech and life science companies in western Pennsylvania. They were the perfect fit.

Once we approached the PLSG leadership for approval and won their support, we now had our primary applicant and the two training entities that would perform the work required by the grant. What was left was the effort to secure as much political and community support for the application as possible.

This meant working with key leaders in the community and

trade organizations that were willing to lend their name and clout to the effort. Our first outreach was to elected officials, in particular on the federal level (as this was a federal grant) to secure letters of support on behalf of the initiative. Getting letters of support from members of Congress often helps your grant efforts. When a grant officer receives your grant application, accompanying it with letters from members at a minimum raises their eyebrows and lets them know the project has the endorsement of the local elected representation, regardless of political affiliation.

Second, we garnered support from local trade groups, universities, and of course our clients and similar companies that would benefit from the grant by sending their employees and prospective employees to the program at no cost for up-skilling and retraining.

One of these groups was the Pittsburgh Technology Council (PTC). The PTC boasted a membership of over 1500 southwestern Pennsylvania tech and biotech companies and was the local "chamber of commerce" for tech-related activity. Luckily for us, we had several friends there.

The PTC's CEO at the time was Steve Zylstra, and his Vice President for Government Affairs was Brian Kennedy. Brian and I had spent a number of years working together at Senator Santorum's office in economic development, and as fate would have it, Brian and Steve's relationship with us bore fruit for our clients becasue they agreed to lend their considerable political gravity to the effort through a letter of support for the grant.

In the end, we submitted the grant through the PLSG, identified the institutions of higher learning that perform the retraining, and we identified legislators and key trade organizations that would lend their political capital in the grant submission – and we hadn't begun to even write the grant. This is the definition of grant development, and one can see how this combines both a domain expertise in understanding what it will take to win a grant with the network of a lobbyist to marshal the resources to be successful in the endeavor. It required a total team effort from our lobbyists and internal grant writers to win for our clients here.

The irony is, in fact, that our clients never touched the money from the grant and were not even the grant applicant when it was finally submitted. However, we successfully secured $2.6 million in federal funding for the creation of this retraining program, and our clients received the financial benefit of sending several hundred employees through the program at no cost. This is the importance of grant development.

- Grant writing is the third step in this process. I would be lying if I said that grant writing was for everyone. It takes a certain patience and attention to detail, as I have seen grants thrown out of the process for arriving in the grant manager's office four minutes late or for using the wrong font as identified in the grant application. Not all grant offices are this rigorous, but all require a level of organization and sophistication to be successful.

Grant writing is often where our clients need us the most. If they didn't have the in-house capacity or time to identify and develop a grant on their own, they often need to buy the hours of our grant writing team to execute on the drafting of the grant itself.

Yes, you can successfully write a grant on your own, but if you have never done so, it may be best to retain the services of a grant professional to help you with the first attempt. However, an erudite person can cobble together a quality grant effort with enough proficiency if they allocate the time.

Grant writing is what it is – it is the drafting, editing and submitting of a grant by the required deadline. Many lobbying shops maintain internal grant writers for these purposes and others subcontract the work to individuals when the need arises for their clients. Others don't provide this service at all.

Grant writing is both an art and a science like many of the services that lobbyists provide. The science part requires the true blocking and tackling of the grant writing itself – following the grant instructions correctly and building a strong argument to win the grant award.

The art of grant writing is much different. Success rests here in the iterative process with clients to get the best understanding possible of what they would like to achieve.

Let's be honest – grant writers are smart people, but they may not understand a sophisticated new technology that you are developing. Therefore, they need to work closely with you and your team to translate a language of high science and new product benefits to the government into the language of "government speak". This isn't always easy.

Because of this, the grant writing component is usually a blend of the lead grant writer's finesse and "word-smithing" ability along with the client's ability to help translate their value proposition into something the government wants to fund.

Grant writing includes drafting statements of need for the grant funding (what purpose the grant will serve), project narratives (how you plan on spending the grant money if received), budgets (again how the money will be spent within the eligible uses of the grant) and completion of the standardized federal and/or state grant forms.

When a notice of funding availability is announced, you will usually have between 30 and 90 days to respond with the average grant response time being 45 days. That may sound like ample time but once you've tried to craft your first grant it will be self-evident that you will need nearly every day of their timeframe to complete the grant on time.

To avoid finding a grant but not having the turnaround time to effectively complete it, I would advise you to create a grant calendar for yourself. This is not necessarily as simple as it sounds, but we at GSP and now DMGS do this for our clients to avoid such pitfalls.

Grant calendaring is the process through which you not only look at grants that are currently available for your organization but also track grants that you may have missed in the current fiscal year. By calendaring a grant that was available last February, you will remind yourself in November that 90 days from now, that grant may be cycling back to you. By looking months ahead to anticipate the release of grants, you won't miss it the next time around.

Why is this effective? Keep in mind that many grants are cyclical. They usually become available on some recurring basis – once a year, once a quarter, etc. Some grants are even available on a "rolling basis" meaning that with the beginning of every fiscal year, the coffers to these programs are replenished and you may apply for a grant at any time during that fiscal year. But when the money runs dry, the program is closed until the start of the next fiscal year.

An accurate grant calendar will help you monitor when grants are usually due to hit the street, and therefore you can plan accordingly to assure that you have the allotted time to draft a competitive response.

One last point on grant writing before we move on to the final step — even though grants appear competitive on the outside, some grants can be decided by external influences. Some grants such as federal SBIR and STTR grants are designed to be peer reviewed and their awards based on merit. However other grants can be helped by the political gravity of relevant legislators.

Allow me to provide a quick example. Some states offer public incentive for companies to grow, retain, expand and relocate their businesses to their state. I am sure you have all read stories where a firm was relocating from one state to another and in return received tax incentives, grants or low-interest loans to help with the relocation process. These grants are often influenced by the Governor or state legislators who will benefit from the company's relocation to their district or state.

The final stage of your grant strategy needs to be grant

administration. Grant administration is the simplest of the four stages to understand but often ends up being complicated in practice.

All grants come with strings. Some are less onerous than others. The motivation for these requirements is fairly straightforward. At its core, government is always concerned with the perception that it is spending taxpayer money poorly. No good bureaucrat wants to spend money on a project that may end up being the focus of some investigative reporter's story, nor does an elected official want to expend political capital on a grant to come back and bite them. Shall we say "Solyndra"?

Therefore, regardless of a grant being of a federal, state or local nature, each program has required eligible uses that garner its administration. These uses more than likely will require a compliance trail of some kind, often including some light auditing responsibilities in which you will be required to adhere. Usually these are items that your CFO or COO can handle, but in some cases it may require an outside accounting firm or legal counsel, depending on the sophistication and the size of the grant.

Some lobbying firms have the internal capacity to help with grant administration. It is not the glory work of this process but it is equally as important as the rest. You do not want to find yourself on the opposite end of an agency inquiry because the funding you received may have been spent inappropriately.

Be prepared to spend time adhering to the grant guidelines of any successful grant you receive, and stay in contact with the agency through which you received it. Don't feel shy about calling and asking for clarification on any guideline, and document conversations when you can through personal notes or email exchanges. Sometimes grant administrators change and the new grant manager may interpret an eligible use of funding differently than the former manager. If you have documentation that you have been approved to use funding in a certain way, this provides some air cover in the event you get caught up in an administrative or policy shift.

Helping Companies Grow

When companies think about government grants, they often just consider the kind of money that may be available for research and development. However, governments, especially at the state and local levels, will subsidize the growth of your business, the expansion of your facilities and the training of your workforce. This type of development is another area of expertise that GSP and now DMGS grew to handle over time to help its customers.

It is also a service that a well-informed CEO of his or her own company can achieve on their own. Our service is called Development Finance Consulting, but for all intents and purposes, it is the strategy and tactics behind securing government funding for everything from site improvements to real estate development.

Development Finance Consulting, or DFC, pertains to devising a tailored strategy for our clients that enables proposed development plans to become successful projects. From commercial real estate development to municipal infrastructure needs to historic preservation plans, DFC marshals the resources of federal, state and local sources of public subsidy for your project.

Most states, county and city governments now compete against one another to land companies that are expanding or relocating their headquarters or new divisions. In return for public subsidy, these companies, in part, entice cities to compete against other cities, counties to compete against other counties and states to compete against other states in return for the capital expenditure they will invest and the new jobs created.

As a result, most state and local governments offer public incentive programs that are triggered by job creation, a relocation of a corporate headquarters or something similar to win over businesses looking to expand or relocate. DFC is our way of describing the process through which companies can avail themselves of these public incentives and offset the costs of their move and expansion.

Beyond private capital, complex development projects often require some form of public funding assistance to fill financial gaps. Your company can identify these sources of funding through a variety of means:

- First, check in with your state's (or the states in which you may want to relocate) economic development department. The names of these agencies vary from state to state but a good Google search will usually lead you directly to their site. From there, you can view the types of funding a state may offer. Usually these come in the form of grants, low interest loans and forms of various tax credit or abatement programs.

- Replicate this for the cities and counties that are also targets for your potential expansion or relocation. Larger counties and cities tend to have more programs to offer than smaller ones, but don't leave any stone unturned in your due diligence.

- Understand that you can compete one location against another. There is no reason that you cannot compete and seek the best offer between states or cities if your expansion is significant enough. Offers from states can range from several thousand to several million depending on the size and scope of the deal.

- Some private firms may also hire specialized site selection firms so that they can remain anonymous and let professionals handle the site selection and business incentive negotiation processes for them. At GSP we uniquely combine the site selection process with lobbying to maximize support from elected officials which often leads to greater commitments from states and cities.

- Be advised that some sites are better than others. Often states and local governments will form targeted zones for reinvestment (usually in blighted areas or in areas where a large mill or business has just left for business reasons). These sites may qualify you for more funding or additional subsidy because of their designation. This is something else to consider when choosing a site.

- Even if you know where you are going or you have the site under control, there's no reason to give up your leverage and tell someone that. Let them compete for your business, and you will maximize your public assistance.

- Understand that many of these programs come with their own hooks – you may be asked to create a certain number of jobs or stay in the state or targeted zone for a period of three to five years. If you don't meet some of these requirements over time, the state or local government usually places "clawback" provisions in their offer letters that will allow them to ask for their money back (or at least some prorated share). Buyer beware!

- The focus of many of these grants usually maintain strict eligible uses. For example, some typical uses are for items such as the costs of public infrastructure (turning lanes, signalization, ingress/egress, telecommunications, water/sewer, extension of utilities, etc.). In other cases, these subsidies can be applied to other costs such as construction of new facilities, renovation or "greening" of existing facilities, workforce development and job training, the purchase of new machinery or equipment and the like.

States and local governments will often ask you to fill out a worksheet which may ask for details on how many employees you may hire over a period of years or ask you to share your projected capital expenditures to make sure you meet their requirements to trigger various programs. Just make sure you don't overestimate as you don't want to find yourself not hitting the goals in the final offer letters from the state or local agencies.

A fairly sizeable example of this kind of work can be described in a case study from one of our former clients, Forest City

Enterprises. FCE was redeveloping an historic train station in the Pittsburgh region called the Station Square Marina and Riverfront Development and they retained the services of GSP to help.

One of our first clients, Forest City came to us when we were still without office space. John was working out of his house, I was working out of mine, and Starbucks functioned as our conference room. We were invited to meet with the project lead, and our job was to point to the artist's renderings and describe ways in which we believed we could help them.

We ended up working for the Station Square developers on a federal, state and local basis. If they had hired one of our competitors they would have had to hire a D.C.-based firm to conduct D.C. lobbying; a Harrisburg firm to do state lobbying; and a local firm to lobby in Pittsburgh and Allegheny County. We did it all for them, which ended up costing them about one-half of what it would have cost had they hired three separate firms through traditional lobbyist platforms.

Station Square is an old train station that was taken over by the Pittsburgh History and Landmarks Foundation back in the 1980s. The History and Landmarks Foundation founded Forest City Enterprises, a Cleveland-based developer, to redevelop Station Square into a multi-tenant riverfront to be used for commercial and entertainment venues. The Station Square project also needed Federal funding for two additional projects: a marina and a pedestrian bridge to span the existing rail lines.

All told, Forest City Enterprises' design was a $72 million

expansion and improvement project that included the new marina, new restaurant and bar spaces, and a riverfront trail. The significant expansion required Forest City to develop complex, multi-modal transportation systems for pedestrian and vehicular access, and on-site amenities.

We first identified and secured $1 million in funding through the U.S. Department of Transportation for a pedestrian bridge and stair tower which would allow visitors river access over permanent rail lines.

The following year, we secured $350,000 from the Commonwealth of Pennsylvania and the Department of Conservation and Natural Resources for a riverfront park and trail along the north shore of the site. In 2004, we secured a $6 million grant from the Commonwealth of Pennsylvania through the Redevelopment Assistance Capital Program (or RACP) for the construction of another pedestrian bridge and walkway connecting Station Square to much-needed parking and public transportation.

Lastly, we helped Forest City secure tax increment financing for the redevelopment of Bessemer Court, an area in which several new restaurants and an outdoor café would be built. All in, we helped Forest City with public subsidies of a combined $20 million. That's $20 million of a $72 million project.

Station Square helped to create an estimated 800 new jobs. It brings tourists to the area who could then take paddle boats, or the water taxi, to see historic sites, to shop or have lunch, etc. It puts heads in hotel beds. In a multitude of ways, the government sees that money come back through taxes and fees, and they were willing to invest in a quality project. The developers just needed some help navigating the government marketplace, and they needed us to show them how to get those dollars.

CHAPTER FOUR:

Disabusing the Negative Image of Lobbyists

The Road Less Traveled

Think about lobbying in these terms. If McDonalds spent millions of dollars every year telling you that Burger King and Wendy's prepare unsafe meals, underpay their employees, provide unclean facilities in which to eat, and overcharge you, would you buy a dinner at either place?

If you answered "no" to this question, you are the victim of negative advertising. It happens every day in the world of politics. I'll bet you can't remember some of the positive advertisements you have seen from the latest and greatest round of political airtime, but I'll bet you can remember that such and such Congressman stole candy from kids and pushed old ladies out of nursing homes.

It's the power of negative advertising, and it has truly given our industry a bad name. Let's face facts. When you think about a lobbyist, what's the first thing that comes to mind? Dumping money into campaigns to re-elect unworthy politicians bought off by the special interests?

If you answered "yes" to this question, then you are validating why I need to pen this section of the book. For all the heartache and media spin you read about our industry, lobbyists provide services necessary to make our government work efficiently. I will try and convince you of this in the next few pages.

As different as we were, I'd be lying if I said that GSP and now DMGS didn't fit some of the cliché lobbying firm stereotypes. As a firm, our team engages in its fair share of client entertainment, treating clients and legislators within the legal guidelines to ballgames, steak dinners and the occasional cigar. However, with the onset of many of the lobbying and campaign finance reform laws passed in the last decade, those marketing efforts have been restricted in many ways in Washington and in almost every state capitol.

But that doesn't mean that we don't actively engage in helping like-minded legislators that support our causes and our clients. We regularly host fundraisers (more than I'd like to admit) but we always viewed this as a necessary part of the job. Raising money for candidates that support your political views is again a right protected by the First Amendment of the U.S. Constitution. In fact, it is an extension of it.

Just as you have the right to place a bumper sticker on your car in support of a candidate or cause, raising money to help candidates that support you and your beliefs is important to ensure that not only is your voice heard, but that you have the right pieces left on the chess board to win the game.

In our business, campaign donations are traditionally made by either individuals or through a Political Action Campaign (PAC). As lobbyists, we will sometimes make contributions through our PAC to support legislators who support our clients. In some cases, you're buying tickets to a legislator's events or hosting events for a legislator. These events provide forums in which you (and/or your clients) can express support for a legislator's re-election campaign.

It is important to note that, regardless of public perception, these events do not provide a forum for *quid pro quo*. In fact, linking campaign events to official business is forbidden in many respects. Inevitably conversations may strike up that blend work with pleasure, but it is incumbent upon the lobbyist to extricate himself or herself from anything that may be deemed inappropriate. There will be time to return to meet with legislators on official business and in proper settings so that the two events are not confused.

Sounds strange, right?

But absolutely true if you are playing by the rules. This is one practice that I explain over and over again to clients because the rules are there but perception is "there are no rules."

Second, lobbyists are by their nature skilled communicators. Many of us have come from the Hill while others make their bones in this business by leaving a campaign or government agency and turning their years of experience or networks into success for their clients.

Unfortunately, you don't hear about the 99 percent of our industry that does yeoman's work and that play within the rules. Just like in every other field, we have some bad apples. But all industries have their versions of unethical players. Other industries enjoy their privacy more and don't live their lives in an environment where they are not so publicly disclosed. Unless they end up in court or on the nightly news, you hear less of their gaffes and almost all of ours.

In the world of lobbying however, it's like living and working in a fishbowl. As registered lobbyists, we are required to publicly disclose much of what we do for our clients. It is this transparency that provides the checks and balances for our actions.

For instance, when I sign a new client I have to disclose that I've signed that client, who they are, how much they are paying me, the issues we're working on, when they hired me, when they either fire me or when I complete their project. This information is made public in Washington D.C. through the Lobbying Disclosure Act (LDA), and is available to anyone interested in looking it up. It's all there and it's all transparent, which is how it should be. That's all the good stuff.

Similar administrative disclosures are often kept at the state and local levels of government as well. The days of the "Wild Wild West" in our industry are over, as all levels of government have adopted some form of lobbying or campaign finance reform over the last decade. The reason all those checks and balances are in place is to keep guys like me from doing the bad stuff – like using money to build a "bridge to nowhere."

The LDA is in place for the purposes of full disclosure and transparency, which enables private citizens and watchdog groups to know what we lobbyists are up to. Our government enacted the Freedom of Information Act for similar reasons.

Like lawyers, lobbyists get a bad rap. But that view depends upon which side of the table you're sitting. The bottom line is that we are trying to influence the outcome for people, or a group of people. When we are working for a group of people and their side wins, it's good, everyone's happy, and we're heroes.

When we are working against that side, we're bad, people are angry and we're evil. A good example showcasing the negative side of lobbying can be found in a project in my hometown of Pittsburgh. It is an example that has been used in everything from presidential debates in 2008 to campaign ads about earmark reform.

A few years ago, several members of Congress from Pennsylvania worked to secure an earmark through the transportation appropriations bill for an extension of the existing subway system from downtown Pittsburgh to the North Shore of the city. Earmarks, or congressionally directed funding, are ways that legislators fund projects in appropriation bills that become law by adding dollars to the bill before final passage for projects in their states or districts.

The project would dig a "chunnel" under the Allegheny River and connect both Center City with the redevelopment of the city's North Side. Many opponents of the project claimed that the subway extension was unneeded and came in over budget. But the truth is, the project does link the city to the North Shore via a continuous subway loop, helping to promote both economic development and community revitalization.

When planners in the 1970s built Three Rivers Stadium on the North Shore, there were articles written about the development potentially being so successful, it may create a "2nd downtown" with vibrant shops and businesses clambering to build their new headquarters next to the stadium. The failure in that development was connectivity, or public transit. The North Shore Connector now provided a solution to that problem.

Yet other opponents claimed that the federal transportation money would have been better spent elsewhere on other projects the city needed. But as few people know, this funding was ONLY available by statute for this type of project.

So, as a legislator, do you accept the funding and bring $600 million in federal money that helped to create a decade's worth of construction, architecture and engineering jobs in the area and help promote transit connectivity to support economic growth in a blighted area of the city – or – do you decline the funding and let some other area of the country spend it?

There are at least two sides to every argument and in this case, the public opinion here was guided by the media and other special interests that opposed its construction. The legislators and lobbyists that worked on the project continue to be excoriated for this wastrel spending. But now that you know the full story, ask yourself the question, what would you do?

Angels and Devils

The fact that lobbyists are always behind the scenes working in the shadows doesn't help our cause. People like to draw conspiracy theories that lobbyists are secretive and manipulative, working behind the curtain to get what their clients want.

From my side of the table, lobbying just isn't like that; it's simply a professional guide to the Hill, the Capitol, or some partner agency, and people are always welcome to take a peek at what we're doing. We are neither angels nor devils. We are simply professionals performing a job like anyone else.

In reviewing our country's political history, one can see that lobbying began the day our forefathers signed the Constitution. This document was specifically designed to create a government that would be slow to change and difficult to consolidate power in one branch of government. The parliamentarian procedures and the separations of power provided by the Constitution and adopted by the U.S. Congress were established to deliberately impede the passage of new legislation, making it a difficult task.

Remember that, at first, our country was just a bunch of states with very little in common. It was difficult to travel between states let alone to Washington to lodge a complaint or support an issue. Hence the dawn of lobbying – or sending someone in your stead to do the work for you.

Our election laws dictate that the vast majority of federal legislators are to be elected every two years. In the past, Congress was to be in session for only short periods, allowing representatives to return to run the family farm during times of harvest, or return to the family business when their term was up. Congress wasn't meant to be a full-time body in America's formative years.

Regardless, the Constitution was created so that there would be external influence in the form of the First Amendment. Unlike living under the rule of the King of England and Parliament, your voice could be heard – either through the legislator representing your district or through your Senators, who at the time were appointed by your Governor.

Our government was formed as a democracy to give individuals that voice and the power that goes with it. We've changed governance over the years, but First Amendment rights – specifically the Right to Free Speech, the right to vote and the right to assemble are all guaranteed. And if the government denies these rights you have the power to protest, to speak out and to speak up. You may defend those rights by force, with the right to bear arms, etc. These very concepts represent the earliest forms of lobbying and date back to the very first days of our government.

Today, lobbying has evolved into an industry much like the legal community. Now that government has become a pervasive part of all of our lives, experts in the lobbying field fill a variety of holes. In times past, the government provided for the common defense and promoted the general welfare of its citizens; it had a standing army and it built a few roads, but all other issues were left to the individual states.

But today's government oversees many more functions of our daily lives than the founding fathers ever anticipated. Lobbyists serve the purpose of being the private government professionals that are aware of where all the pieces fit in the puzzle.

Left, Right and Somewhere In Between

You've got Republicans. You've got Democrats. You've got people and businesses on both sides of the political aisle, and also those who reside somewhere in between. How do you get everyone to work across party lines peacefully? Answer is, you don't.

For example, on one side, there are groups that think big business runs everything and deregulation will yield more pollution. On the other side, you'll hear that cap and trade is bad because these new rules will put U.S. companies at a disadvantage to foreign companies that don't have to follow the same onerous regulations, and therefore we're going to lose jobs to offshore locations that don't care about cap and trade. Opposing views are important and the truth lies somewhere in the middle.

Yes, there is a need for regulation so that industry doesn't hurt people or do something unthinkable like unleash harmful chemicals that cause cancer. And yes, it is also true that business needs to be unshackled in order to enable companies to do what they do best, which is to generate wealth and create jobs.

It is this middle ground – this in between – for which lobbyists are always fighting. Of course there are also extremists on both sides of the equation. They're not moving the needle, but they are making problems for the people in the middle who are trying for some kind of reform. This is the kind of thinking that lobbyists have to overcome on a day to day basis; arguments from the far left or far right that live on the fringe of the political spectrum being fought so that neither side has to move one step closer to the middle. Most legislators recognize it for the rhetoric it is, and simply put it aside and yet, it is one more reason for the increased polarization of our government that often results in preventing any kind of resolution.

Special Interest Groups

Right off the bat, let's debunk the idea that lobbyists are hijacking Washington and keeping people's voices from being heard in favor of special interest groups. Nothing could be further from the truth. Like Robin Hood, from time to time when I lobby,

I fight for the little guy – I give him or her a voice. And what is true is that a single voice doesn't usually make a difference; but if an association of folks comes together to lobby as a group, together they can certainly affect change in D.C.

A Chamber of Commerce, on balance, represents pro-business ideals. But even the Chamber of Commerce has competing interests from within. There are those members who want to promote small business and they tend to be paranoid and sometimes fight against big business interests. Those who promote big business are sometimes seen as bullies, trying to push out the little guy. A lobbyist's job is to protect the interests of their client and make these internal fissures disappear so the group may act as one. There is more power in the voice if they stand united.

At GSP and now DMGS, we advocate for and protect our clients. Those who say that lobbying is in some way unethical or try to demonize our profession simply don't understand the process. As citizens of this country, you need to participate in government just as you need to exercise your right to vote. Our government was founded on the democratic principle that you do have a vote, that it's a precious vote and a privilege, and you need to exercise the right to vote regardless of whether or not you think it's a waste of time. Voting is the most basic form of lobbying that we do, except our profession is executed in Washington or Harrisburg or Sacramento where there are people voting in a democratic republic. As a lobbyist, it is important to tell your legislators what your clients want. If you do not, they're going to vote however they see fit. This may not be optimal or fit your clients or their ideals. Remember, at the end of all this, if legislators aren't supporting your positions, you can vote them out next time around. If you exercise your right to vote, that is.

In terms of special interest groups, let's say you're a Congresswoman and you need to know everything there is to know about health care reform for a vote that is approaching. The American Medical Association visits you for the purpose of educating you on their positions. When they leave, the American Dental Association comes in and gives you their version of things. Finally the Chamber of Commerce comes in and educates you as well about how the passage of this bill will impact businesses in your district.

You listen politely to each group's ideas about health care reform and, if you took to heart all of the recommendations and made all of the changes each group requested, it's easy to envision a scenario where the bill becomes unaffordable or unworkable.

For this reason, as a Congresswoman, you have to make decisions based on what you believe. You probably didn't come from a medical background; you may not understand how Medicare and Medicaid work in the scenarios presented in the new bill; perhaps you don't understand how Social Security affects this or that, and you've got to learn everything on the fly. Finally, when your congressional leadership comes to you and says, "I don't care what they said, I need you to vote this way," you've got to make those tough decisions in an informed manner. This poses a dilemma; what do you do? This is why lobbying is important.

In the end, the Congresswoman will likely vote for or against the bill depending on which group did the best in educating her, spending the time to visit her in the office and advocating for their position most effectively. If someone hasn't taken that time to visit her, she may not have the expertise or the knowledge to vote for their position or be uncomfortable justifying her vote.

So, are special interest groups running the country? Not necessarily. But if your interests are not represented in Washington or your state capitols, then your voice will not be heard.

Smoke and Mirrors

Someone recently asked me whether all of government was just smoke and mirrors. If a legislator is supposed to be an expert on hundreds of different topics, but has to get that information from other people, he or she doesn't really know anything. Well, to some extent this is true. No single legislator can keep abreast of the staggering amount of new information they receive each day. That is why legislative staffers exist. Remember in the beginning of this book when I said I was a young buck earning no money but making big decisions? That's the way it is in Washington, and it is these staffers who help to shape decision-making in Washington.

A staffer's – or legislative assistant's – job is to manage certain issue areas for their member of Congress. Usually this means a House or Senate staffer is assigned seven or eight legislative topics to cover. Legislators depend on these staffers to help monitor bills related to these topic areas, read and interpret legislation and the parliamentarian processes that surround them, work with relevant constituent groups to ensure that the legislator is hearing from voters in his or her district, and respond to constituent inquiries as they arise.

So when the legislator, who's off doing 20 different things, returns and asks for an update on an issue or advice on how to vote on a bill, the staffer has up-to-the-minute information to provide. He or she can make a recommendation based on criteria set by the legislator contemplating congressional leadership requests, the number of constituent calls and inquiries for or against a bill, etc. It's just a recommendation, mind you. The ultimate decision is up to the legislator to make, although he or she is depending greatly on the staffer.

When I was a staffer, at the end of each day, the Senator would get a verbal or written report about the type and frequency of constituent calls and letters. If there was an inordinate amount of calls or letters that day on a certain subject area, it would tip us off to issues of import to our constituency and provide us the public opinion we may need to make an informed vote. Usually these high volume periods would correspond to big budget votes or current events covered by the daily news.

As a lobbyist, my job is to make sure the staffer has all the information available when it comes time for them to make that recommendation to their boss. In terms of relationship management, staffers are often equally as important as legislators. You may only get five minutes with a legislator, but if he or she says to send the information to their staffer, then you know it will get discussed again before it is time for a vote.

As innocuous as it may sound, this is where I learned a very important lesson in the art of public service and understood that

I needed to imbed similar principles in client service into my business to be successful.

On one of my many trips driving in the hinterlands of Pennsylvania with the Senator, he told me a story of why he put such a premium on constituent service. He told me when he was a freshman Congressman, he had a discussion with then Speaker of the House, Tip O'Neill.

Tip and Rick couldn't be farther apart on the political spectrum – a rugged individualist like Rick defending the conservative Republican battle lines, and a longtime, experienced liberal Democrat from Massachusetts, defending his ideals in Tip. Politics aside, they both recognized the need for public service.

Rick approached Tip for some advice as a young representative. For some time, Rick's district offices would receive calls from constituents complaining that their street light was out or they had a pothole in their neighborhood. As a federal official, Rick was two layers of governance removed from directly being able to help. These were jobs for the Mayor of their town or a public works department.

So Rick asked the veteran Democrat how he handled those calls.

Tip confided that you and your staff handle all of those calls as if it were your mother calling you. You don't refer them to the Mayor, you get on the phone with them and call the Mayor about the street light or pothole yourself. You don't politely give them the number for the public works department, your staff calls the department for them.

In Tip's advice to the Senator came the same wisdom I used to create GSP. Constituent service, or in our case customer service, is everything.

These people were calling the Congressman because they knew him, trusted him or thought he could help. And by giving a little tender lovin' care on the phone with them to their Mayor, he would fulfill his duty as a public servant.

So, is it all smoke and mirrors? Not really. But through staff and being an active and strong public servant, this underscores how legislators are able to stay so well informed on issues.

Media Influence

When you charge the field with trumpets blaring, be prepared because the cameras will be rolling. As they say in the news, "if it bleeds it leads." From a press perspective, anything negative, regardless of how large or small, may get media attention. If I make a mistake in my life, no one cares. I'm just some guy. But an elected official is always under a public microscope, and making a mistake means paying the consequences.

Here's a little story to illustrate what I mean. When I was 22, I was working for Congressman Rick Santorum. As a form of job preservation, I was also volunteering my nights and weekends doing work for his U.S. Senate campaign bid. At the time, Pennsylvania was represented by Senator Harris Wofford. Wofford was the Clinton presidential darling because he supported most of Clinton's big issues including the embattled and controversial universal health care legislation; if Wofford fell, it would mean that the 1994 watershed Republican revolution could claim the Senate as well as the House. These were the famous days of the Newt Gingrich "Contract with America" election cycle and a win in Pennsylvania, which was a very blue state, could turn the Senate to majority Republican red.

So Clinton sent Paul Begala and James Carville to Pennsylvania to make sure Rick didn't win. Part of the strategy employed was to have someone follow Rick around, from event to event, recording him with a camera and boom microphone, waiting for something negative to present itself.

What came out of it was a negative ad we dubbed the infamous "Social Security" ad, which their campaign dropped two weeks before the election in order to elicit maximum damage. The ad was taken from a speech Santorum gave at a college in northwestern Pennsylvania. A young woman asked whether she'd ever see any of her Social Security benefits if things didn't change and what the Congressman, if elected to the Senate, would do to protect her benefits.

As the cameras rolled Rick answered the question honestly by saying there were a couple things that could be done. First, he offered that the federal government could increase the retirement age from 65 to 75; or as another solution the government could perhaps cut benefits to retirees. Lastly he said taxes could be raised to make up the gap when the baby boomer generation retires as there will be fewer people working to support more beneficiaries.

An honest answer from an honest guy. The other side took that two-minute answer and edited it together in a way that made

Rick look like he intended to raise the age for Social Security and cut benefits, literally blasting him in the week before the election. As a result, Rick lost double-digit points in his lead of Wofford and for a short duration remained nearly five points down.

To fight back, Rick's campaign team turned the tables on the Wofford team, as we began to film the guy who had been following the Congressman around filming him. The Santorum camp cut a response ad showing the dirty political tricks the Wofford campaign had engaged in to smear the Congressman's record. Once the electorate saw the dirty pool, the negative ad began to backfire and the Congressman recovered and won the election by only a handful of points. It was a long night, but it ended happily.

The Good, the Bad, the Ugly

The Good

I mentioned earlier that lobbying, like many industries, sees a full spectrum of issues and people – some of which are fair and favorable, others of which are not so nice. Our job is to make sure our clients play fair and defend them from those who seek to stop their projects or change a piece of policy that may hurt them.

One example of lobbying done the "good" way is a project we engaged in for two clients working together for a common cause. Coca Cola hired GSP when the Pittsburgh Steelers and the Green Bay Packers were playing against one another in the 45th Superbowl. Around the same time, Coke was launching a new bottle design. They wanted to promote the new bottle and part of the challenge was to get people to go to their website and click on the link that would promote the new design.

Our role, along with a similar outfit in Green Bay, was to work with Coke to encourage folks to visit the website or mention the challenge through social media. If each city got a targeted 1,000 hits to the website, Coke would make a donation of $10,000 to the Boys & Girls Club in each city, and this donation would be presented by the Governor of that state. Luckily for us, the Boys & Girls Club in Pittsburgh is called the Sarah Heinz House and they, too, were a client of GSP.

Using a grassroots effort through the kids at the Club and our own networks, GSP was able to gather the requisite number of hits needed, as both the cities won the challenge money.

To take it one step further, the Governors of each state were to make a bet that, whichever team won, the loser would wear the opposing team's jersey while presenting the check to the Boys & Girls Club. Unfortunately for Steeler Nation, Green Bay won the game.

Newly elected Pennsylvania Governor Tom Corbett made his first press stop back to the Pittsburgh area just after the Superbowl loss and lived up to his side of the bargain. Begrudgingly he wore a Packers jersey during the check presentation and joked with the kids about the vices of gambling getting you in trouble sometimes but that you should always live up to your bets.

In the end, this is a great story for Coca Cola, a great story for the kids at Sarah Heinz House and a story that underscores how lobbying can be done in a "good" way. Clint Eastwood would have been proud.

The Bad

Good cannot exist without "bad" and I wanted to leave you with a story that exemplifies the "Lee Van Cleef" of lobbying. When I was working with Senator Santorum in the mid-1990s, part of my job was to prioritize and rank projects that the Senator may want to help in 36 of the 67 counties in Pennsylvania. At the time, I oversaw economic development activities from Harrisburg to Pittsburgh to Erie, which represented about three–fifths of the state geographically.

During one of our appropriation cycles, I was visited by a lobbyist to discuss his project list. After receiving it, I noticed that he represented both a county and a city within the same region and was asking for funding for both. The projects would have to come out of the same bucket of money and I knew that I would only be able to fund one of the two. In effect, he had competing interests.

When I told him that I likely would only have funding available for one of the two projects, he softly giggled and said "give it to the county, they pay me more."

In part, it is from this horrible story that I derived the business model for GSP.

The Ugly

This one is so awful, it's hard for me to put in the book or believe it wouldn't make Eli Wallach turn his head away.

We were representing a nonprofit organization in a no-longer-prosperous inner city area. The nonprofit was working to create a business incubator out of one of the old buildings that was being renovated. They were using green energy to rebuild, and had a great and active board of directors that was trying to help revitalize the local economy.

GSP was hired to find federal and state funding for the project, and got them $750,000 from the state grant for workforce development and a $500,000 earmark from the federal government to help with ingress and egress issues to and from the site. One afternoon, we received a call from the director of the organization stating that he had some surprising but welcomed news – the Mayor of the city was going to present the project with a check for $5 million to help match the efforts of the state and federal government investment.

I had to say I was stunned. GSP wasn't hired to do any local lobbying – just the state and federal piece– so we hadn't heard about the local funds until the last minute. Keep in mind that the purpose of the nonprofit retaining us was to find funding to train and retrain dislocated workers who had lost their jobs in the economic downturn and help educate and retrain Welfare-to-Work moms so they could find jobs. It was a major win in the fight to rebuild this city.

Soon afterwards, we received word from the city that the Mayor wanted to call a press conference at our client's facility and present this generous check; the press, the board members and representatives from the incubator businesses were invited as well. Never missing an opportunity to secure some earned media for our cause and client, we quickly mobilized to help prepare for the event.

The day of the event went off without a hitch as we gathered friends and colleagues under a tent in preparation for the Mayor's arrival. The event was covered by much of the local media outlets and things were running smoothly. Now all we needed was the Mayor.

So we waited…and waited…and waited. After 30 minutes, we started to call the Mayor's office and staff to find out how long the delay was going to be as the press began to get antsy. Soon after the calls went out, a limousine rolled into the parking lot, and we thought the Mayor was ready to go.

Instead, emerging from the limousine stepped one of the Mayor's economic development guys with a big mock check for $5 million - but the Mayor was nowhere to be found. The staffer made his way out onto the stage and the event proceeded as planned. The light bulbs went off; the cameras rolled; the speeches and thank you's commenced. From the side of the stage all went well and the client appeared happy.

As the press trucks began to leave and the crowd began to disperse, I walked onto the stage to congratulate my client on a job well done. As I approached, I saw him shaking hands with the Mayor's staffer and watched the Mayor's guy lean in real close and whisper, "This isn't a check for $5 million. It's a check for $1 million and if you complain, it's a check for $0 million." Then he shakes his hand and quickly returns to his limousine, leaving my stunned client holding a mock check.

The Mayor "out-and-out" lied. He wanted to look good in the eyes of the public and to the press, but he never had the money to give. In the end, I'm certain the organization never saw any money from the city. They had to retool and overhaul their plans in order to make the project work. From my perspective, we were successful in getting them state and federal funding, which helped greatly, but being promised that enormous sum and getting nothing, that, my friend, was ugly.

CHAPTER FIVE:

A Step-by-Step Guide to Lobbying

A Step-by-Step Guide to Lobbying

So, you need to do some lobbying, but can't afford to hire someone to help you. Let's go through some of the basic steps to get you started.

Identifying the Desired Outcome

The first and most important thing is determining the issue at hand. You can't go walking willy-nilly into a legislative office; you can't go knocking on the Governor's door or ringing the bell at the White House; so pin down what it is you want to accomplish well in advance of any and all meetings. Decide what is important to you, what is important to your business or organization and the reasons for doing what you're doing.

We encourage all of our clients to streamline the process by putting together a white paper outlining these elements. A white paper is lobbyist slang for a one- to-two page document that succinctly and lucidly describes who you are, the purpose of your visit to that particular legislator's office, the desired outcome of the meeting backed by facts as to why a legislator should take action on your behalf. Finally, make sure to include accurate contact information for yourself and others so that legislators and their staff may follow up with you when it is time for them to take action on your behalf.

White papers serve several purposes. First, they are a good outline or "cheat sheet" for you to use when you have your 15 minutes with an elected official. It helps neophytes in this process start the conversation and stay on point as legislators have finite windows in their daily calendars. It may sound like hyperbole, but the average legislator on a session day takes anywhere from 15 to 30 meetings, most lasting ten to fifteen minutes. By following along with the outline you will stay on point and on message, and the brevity of the white paper will help you stay within your given time allocation. A cardinal sin is making a legislator late for another meeting because you were unprepared or verbose.

One note on the language you choose to use in your white papers – please translate your message into the language of a legislator, or what we call "political speak." The purpose of this translation is to describe your issue in a more government friendly way or by citing examples of something a legislative officer or an elected official is going to understand and react to more readily.

For instance, rather than saying that you need money to open an organic farm stand because it's good for the environment, you highlight the fact that you're going to hire 10 people once you open. Now you're talking the legislator's language. He or she should be more willing to help you because that's 10 new jobs in his or her district. If you think like the legislator, you'll know how to couch your argument better.

Legislators and government appointees to departments and agencies rarely think in the same terms as those of us in the private sector. If your message to your legislative target speaks to items more important to your investors like wealth generation or how you plan to exit your company, legislators may not fully appreciate the impact you are having in their district.

Legislators are smart people but like most, care about what's important to them (and their district of course.) Hearing that your exit strategy may include the sale of your company to an out of state entity may scare them, as they may interpret that as jobs fleeing their state. But if you spin your argument to talk about job creation or economic impact to their districts instead, now they will readily understand your argument and hopefully help you out with your "ask." In other words, think about how your product, service, or issue will impact the legislator you're going to see. What will make him or her motivated to help you?

Advocating For Your Needs – Legislative Champions

It is important to remember that your local elected officials are there as your legislative representation. You put them into office and now your job is to get to know them and convince them to work as your advocates in D.C., your state capitol or at city hall. There is no good reason that a business person or director of a non-profit organization should not at least have an introductory relationship with their Mayor, their council people at the city and county level, their state House member, state Senate member, the local regional Governor's representative, U.S. House members, and the staffs of the U.S. Senate members representing your state.

If you do this, you now have legislators who are invested in your projects – who have told you where they stand on your issue. You've advocated for yourself and can rely on your legislator to be a champion for you. They support your issue; they understand your business; and they're going to vote the right way on a bill or a budget so that you get the contract.

When an issue comes up for them, they'll be in contact as you're now part of the close group of people they will depend upon in the community. Whether it's an issue that affects homeless kids, or the way you're delivering services at a food bank, they'll call you because they see you as a leader.

In order to solidify these relationships, I suggest a number of ideas for your organization:

- First, I recommend you plan a legislative open house hosted at your facility once a year or at least once every two years. This open house is designed to host legislators that represent you, legislators that serve on a particular committee of interest to you, and/or key staff and department and agency personnel that you plan on doing business with on a regular basis.

When forming your invite list, think about the government officials that would benefit most from seeing your facilities and meeting your employees firsthand to discuss your company, your mission and your goals. Sometimes even legislators themselves will help "co-host" your event if appropriate.

Keep the open house simple. Make sure it runs no longer than 90 minutes and be prepared to offer a succinct PowerPoint presentation in the beginning of the event to enforce your key points and message. Make sure you have pre-made packets including physical copies of your presentation for each attendee and any pertinent collateral material you would like to give to them.

Make sure they have a chance to tour your facility and meet your employees or those that you serve. For profit organizations often have facilities conducive to photo opportunities where legislators and staff can take pictures and interact with employees. These photo opportunities may make it into their printed newsletters to constituents or become content for their website.

Last, make sure to end on time and send thank you letters to each attendee for their time and consideration. As I have mentioned before, it's important to respect a legislator's time, and these are small but important tokens of gratitude that show you care and appreciate their support.

- Next, make sure you visit legislators on their own turf once a year if not more. You can do this by arranging your own D.C. or State Capitol Hill days. I would suggest you coordinate trips for you and your executives to meet your legislators and their staffs during session.

These trips serve multiple purposes. First, it reminds elected officials that you care enough and are important enough to travel to meet with them at the Capitol to discuss your issues. Many legislators and staff get caught up in a phenomenon called the "Beltway Mentality" which loosely translated means "if you aren't important enough to come and see me, you aren't important enough for me to worry about." Breaking that mentality by showing up at their door to discuss your issues will surely help.

Second, these trips serve as reinforcement for the message you delivered at your open house and vice versa. Remember, education and advocacy will win the day. The more they hear your message, the more it will resonate. And as a sidebar to this, legislative staffs turn over often so ongoing education is critical.

- Remember to educate and advocate with the legislative staff in the district offices of elected officials. Unlike many of the government affairs firms that focus solely on garnering the support of Capitol Hill staffers (or their equivalents in the state capitol) GSP and now DMGS always recognizes that reaching out to local and district staffers remains a vital part of your advocacy campaign.

I know this to be true because I myself am a former district staffer and was charged with helping the Senator prioritize projects back in the state for the Capitol Hill staff that got the bills passed. Missing a chance to pick up an ally in a local office is yet another cardinal sin that some of our competitors overlook.

- Focus on coalition building. What does this mean? It means it is harder for a legislator to say "no" to five people rather than one and harder to say "no" to thirty people rather than five. Most successful advocacy strategies incorporate support from local businesses, local elected officials and various other stakeholders that have an interest in the success of a request or project. So in addition to your own personally directed efforts, you should coordinate calls and letters of support from key community, business and thought leaders to augment your advocacy strategy.

Hiring a group like GSP or DMGS naturally helps to build broad coalition support much more quickly than doing it on your own as groups like ours have pre-established relationships with a variety of special interest groups already. However, if you are doing this on your own, recognize that you can leverage like-minded community and industry leaders to help you win your advocacy battle.

- Once you have put checks in the boxes of this punch list, you will start to determine who your legislative champions will be and how they can help you solve your government problem. As discussed earlier, champions typically serve on a relevant legislative committee, represent your organization geographically or have known personal interests in a certain issue. Ideally and over time, you will identify champions in D.C., your state capitol and among your city and county elected officials that will be helpful to your effort or cause.

It is important to recognize that legislative champions can and should be from both major parties as your issues need to be important and self-evident regardless of partisan politics. You may need to address your issues with legislators differently because of their political bend but in the end, is job creation a Democratic issue or a Republican one? Trick question…it's both.

Champions can be deployed in a variety of ways. In part, they can help you with general intelligence gathering and bill monitoring. If they know that you are looking for a certain notice of funding availability, they can help you track grants. If you need a sponsor on a bill, perhaps they will be the primary sponsor and lobby for you to secure other co-sponsors to your effort. They and their staff will provide valuable credibility and add strength to your entire comprehensive government strategy. To use a chess term, they will be your knights, rooks and bishops.

- Be issue aware. What I mean by that is straightforward – there are always certain political considerations or political realities that need to be identified as you launch your advocacy campaign. Regional campaigns, local news, national news, policy or power shifts like swearing in a new Speaker of the House will change your political reality. These are all factors to closely monitor as they will undoubtedly influence your campaign and you may need to modify your strategy and approach accordingly.

One real life example of this came to us a few years ago when the late U.S. Senator Arlen Specter switched parties in an attempt to win a general election in the fall. Specter was a longtime moderate Republican and his primary opponent, Pat Toomey, found support in the Pennsylvania Republican party from right of center, endangering Arlen's chances to win the party's nomination. The party switch seemed to many as innocuous because it wasn't uncommon for Arlen to vote with the other team. But to our clients it was more than impactful.

Specter as a Republican was chair of the powerful Senate Appropriations Subcommittee on Labor, Health & Human Services and Education. This appointment afforded him considerable oversight on funding for organizations like schools, colleges, universities, hospitals, clinics, workforce investment boards and the like. When Arlen switched to the Democrats, he lost this key Chairmanship (among other things) and with his demotion to the back bench, Pennsylvania entities that received funding on an annual basis from Senator Specter were negatively impacted with the loss of his clout in D.C.

Tailoring Your Own Government Affairs Strategy

GSP and DMGS have devised dozens of successful and effective government affairs strategies for our clients over the years. While each client demands a tailored, unique approach to their issues, there are certain fundamental steps your organization can follow to help you be more effective in your government efforts:

- First, conduct a strengths and needs analysis of your own organization. What does this mean? Get your internal leadership together and get a better understanding of what you need government to do for you and consider not only your current ongoing activities but also put together a "wishlist" of projects that require public sector attention. Your goals will be ever-changing, and knowing what you want to accomplish will help you set your priorities for your own advocacy efforts.

- Conduct program research. Again what does this mean? What I am suggesting here is that before pursuing a grant or contract capture campaign that you closely monitor the federal and state budgets to understand what may be available to you, whether or not you are on the right vendor lists to receive RFPs, grant notifications, etc. Understand what will be available and what is available currently before deciding on the right strategy of pursuit.

- Messaging is always the key element when approaching the government or elected officials. For any organization, answering the following questions is critical: will this project create jobs, save lives, save taxpayer dollars, increase the efficiency of government and its services, lower health care costs, etc.? You will need to frame an effective message and develop that one page white paper that we discussed earlier. Your messaging must accommodate a government audience.

Barriers to Entry

As in any industry, going in blind is never a wise thing to do. Education and familiarity are your best weapons. In the case of government, the biggest barrier to entry is fear. Fear that it's too complicated, that you don't understand it, that it's slow, that there are strings attached to the money you may receive, that technology or product secrets may be exposed, or the overriding fear that government is just bad for business.

The problem is, sometimes you can get in trouble when you don't do anything.

Let me give you an example. Say you have an idea for a new initiative but you are unclear on how a certain government agency may react. There is no harm in launching a preemptive strike and contacting that agency before you begin taking action and asking for clarification on their statutes, regulations or simply how they would react to the effort. There's no penalty for that. You have a plan to do something a certain way. But they say, "Don't do it that way, do it this way." By reaching out in advance, you're heading off problems at the pass and maybe saving yourself a considerable amount of time and money.

Also, if you need help clearing these barriers, imagined or real, there are government affairs groups like GSP or DMGS in almost every major market; Washington, D.C.; and all state capitols. Don't be shy in asking someone for a meeting and pick their brain about your issue, their costs, the time commitment they will need from you up front to be successful, and most of all, your biggest fears. In many cases, these professionals are discreet and are willing to listen at no cost to you.

FAQs

For the DIY crowd, I frequently encounter the same questions over and over again. I'll spare you the time and expense of emailing or calling me to ask them by trying to predict the questions you may have as you embark on your own lobbying efforts:

Q1: Do you really need to raise money for candidates and their campaigns to be effective in politics?

A1: No, you don't. Lots of civic-minded elected officials don't play the game of *quid pro quo*. They want to help you as much as you need the help. That's their charge as they hold office – to help their constituents.

If you feel like you want to keep them in office because they've helped you, that is your choice. Cut them a check, put a sign in your yard and vote for them. But if you want to keep the division between "church and state" feel free not to engage financially.

I won't lie, fundraising for a candidate will be received positively but in no way is it (or should it be) a requirement for doing business in D.C. or any state capitol.

Q2: As a DIY lobbyist or a novice at the political game, what is the biggest pitfall to avoid?

A2: Know what it is you are asking for and be clear about it. In many cases, if you don't know the parliamentary procedures, the legislative calendar or even how you can be successful in your effort, most elected officials and their staffs will help guide you through. But if they don't know what you are asking for, you will get overlooked.

That's why having an agenda for each meeting, pertinent and accurate leave-behind material and a lucid "ask" is important in every meeting with legislators.

Q3: The public perception of politicians is that they are "sleazy" or "liars." How can I trust that they will help me?

A3: First of all, I don't call elected officials "politicians" – ever. The term "politician" delivers a connotation of someone untrustworthy and/or unethical. Most elected officials are very good, very honest people that unfortunately get millions of dollars spent against them by their opponents and special interest groups every two years on TV and radio telling you how bad they are.

In fact, I find 90 percent of elected officials are among the most honest people I know. This may surprise you but in my realm, we trade almost solely on our word. If I convince an elected official to support a project, I better darn well make sure that project works or else they may not support the next one. The same holds true for them. If they tell me that they are going to vote for my bill and they don't, they can't hide from it. My client knows, I know and their supporters know.

In part this is true because our business is so transparent, regardless of whichever side of the table you sit. But in most cases, elected officials are good people that have sacrificed family and private life for the life of public service. That takes character, and regardless of whether you agree or disagree with an elected official, you have to respect what they and their families are giving up to serve their community.

That said, there are those, as in every profession and walk of life, who cannot be trusted. You will have to discern that on a case-by-case basis and do your best to steer clear of their offices.

Q4: Have you ever made a mistake and misrepresented something and had to address it with a legislator?

A4: Yes. Projects change over time. Messages change too. Sometimes your client has to alter their position because of some new political reality like a budget crunch or changes in leadership from within their organization. It will be incumbent upon you to be honest and timely with this news to legislators who are spending their time and often their political capital to secure a victory for you.

And if you find out you have made a mistake, own up to it. Legislators are people too, and we all make mistakes. Theirs just happen to occur in the "fishbowl" I described earlier.

Q5: Are there times when government assistance is more of a hindrance than a help?

A5: Absolutely. In terms of government funding, sometimes it is offered with "hooks." Just like with investors, government wants something in return for its money. Sometimes it is a requirement to hire a certain number of people. Other times for their investment, they want a commitment from your company to stay in their state for five years. Even other times, they will invest money in your research and development but if you go out of business, they have the right to take the intellectual property or the product you were developing and develop it themselves.

Every program is different and be advised of the "hooks" before you sign any offer letter from a state or government entity.

However, let me be straight – the government isn't in the business of putting your company out of business. The Governor doesn't want to read in the morning papers that because their department of economic development activated its clawback provisions from a grant or low interest loan program that a constituent company's doors closed and 60 jobs were lost. That's bad for everyone.

Usually if you are off pace on the government requirements for a grant or loan, the department or agency offering the loan will grant you additional time to comply. However, don't commit to creating 100 jobs in three years when you know you are only going to create 10.

Be smart about it.

Q6: Is it appropriate to allow a legislator to "take credit" for helping your company or organization?

A6: Of course! Keep in mind that if a legislator helps you with funding for your new building, they should be invited to come and stick the first shovel in the ground or cut the ribbon when it is time to open the doors. Nothing inappropriate about it – and in fact, it will likely endear that legislator to you and your cause.

However, be careful not to commit to naming the building after the legislator or something as permanent as that. It could backfire one day.

Q7: If asking the government for help is so appropriate, why doesn't everyone do it?

A7: Asking the government for assistance is VERY appropriate and every business, no matter how big or small, should bake some form of government affairs into their business plans.

Government impacts our lives on a daily basis, in ways that many don't even consider. Your children are bussed to school because of government. Your trash is collected because of government. You receive electricity, gas and water to your homes through public utilities because of government. It's just hard to think of government in that pervasive way.

And not every business is going to find themselves eligible for grants like in many of the examples I have given, but all businesses interface with government. If you own a bakery and you need parking or "streetscaping" to make your block more aesthetically pleasing to your customers, you need to interact with government. If you are a non-profit organization and you need transit so your low-income customers can reach your services, you need to interact with government. If you are a big business and you need permits for your next expansion, you need to interact with government.

Don't think of government affairs as just finding a subsidy for your growth or some technical aspect of some far reaching policy for your industry. Government touches your business every day from affecting health care costs to sales tax to helping your customers reach you by road, transit or turning lane.

One of my business partners, Amy Kaminski, once quipped that our tagline should be, "GSP – Redirecting the Waste."

As funny as that is, it's partially true. Government isn't the most efficient body and does from time to time waste money. But a strong government affairs plan can help redirect that effort efficiently by continuing to educate local elected officials on your priorities and being that "squeaky wheel" that's going to get the government "oil."

Government is There to Help You

Elected officials get re-elected by doing things well for their constituents. Whether it's bypassing the right type of bills that help their district or helping a constituent with a problem they are having with the Veterans Administration, it's as basic as that.

Sometimes we only see elected officials in D.C. that are in leadership, or you only hear from the Governor of your state or the Speaker of the House because they are the mouthpieces for your party. But what people forget about are all the other rank-and-file representatives who are behind the scenes, those who are there for a reason. Maybe they ran for School Board because their kids were in school and they didn't think something was right. Perhaps they became addicted to the political process and ran for the State House because they want to reform something.

They're impassioned enough to open themselves up to the public criticism that comes from being an elected official. You have to love your country enough to air your dirty laundry in front of everybody. Just as lobbyists are tasked with huge levels of transparency, when you throw your hat into the political ring, there is an enormous amount of pressure on you and your family. You have to be committed 100 percent to run for office, and you must be willing to open your life up to that level of scrutiny.

As an elected official, you are literally waiting for your opponents to take a swing at you. You've got to have enough of a thick skin to say, "I don't care what they say, I'm going to do the right thing," and 90 percent of elected officials are there doing the right thing. You might not agree with it. You might be impassioned about an issue to which I am diametrically opposed, but I have to respect your passion. You say, "I may not be with you on this issue, but I'll vote with you on another one, and we're going to come together where we can."

It's that kind of coalition building that cascades down to the way an elected official offers constituent service. They're there because they want to improve the ballpark that your sons and daughters play in, or they want to build that new fire station and get you that new fire truck, or put computers in the police cars.

Keep this in mind when you approach your legislators. Almost all believe in the nobility of the public service into which they have entered.

So many times, the good things elected officials do are simply overlooked. When I was working for Senator Santorum, I served for nearly three-and-a-half years as his Military and Veterans Affairs Director. In that role, my job was to work on issues of import to the military community statewide in Pennsylvania and serve one of the largest veteran populations per capita in the country. The Senator sat on both the Veterans Affairs Committee and the Armed Services Committee so my work was never done.

During that time, my neighbor, Bill Connors, approached me for help. Bill, a lifelong Democrat and not someone very fond of my boss politically, asked me if I could assist him through my role with the Senator. He had earned a Purple Heart during his service in World War II, and he never received the actual medal. When he was younger, it didn't bother him but as he got older and thought often of his own legacy, he wanted the medal as a reminder and memento for his grandkids and perhaps their grandkids.

I went to the Senator with the request and we quickly penned a letter to our legislative liaison at the U.S. Department of Veterans Affairs. Six weeks later he received the long overdue Purple Heart. I remember taking it to him personally and the great joy and gratitude he expressed upon receiving it.

He passed away recently at the age of 88. When I arrived to pay my last respects, his family had all of his military awards and medals on display at his funeral. It was in that moment that I realized how important such a simple task was to make a veteran and lifelong friend eternally grateful. The family will never forget what the Senator did for their dad.

And although we joke about it from time to time, I'll bet that they became shadow Santorum fans. Sometimes I wonder if he ever secretly strayed from his own party ranks and cast a silent vote for my old boss. In the end, whether he did or didn't isn't the issue. It's just one example of how good people elected to office are there to help, regardless of party. They are public servants above all else.

Playing in the Sandbox

Selling yourself and your project to government takes work. You have to make sure you're representing yourself honestly, that you're not overstating your position, you're not overestimating your "ask," and that you can support your requests with accurate information.

If you apply for a grant, the agency receiving your application will want to see your financials and ensure you can execute on the grant's mission. It is difficult for any government entity to award funding to someone that may be a risk. Keep in mind that government agencies are supposed to be good stewards of public funding and as such will be less likely to give money or contracts to high-risk vendors. It is not in the government's best interests to award dollars in any form to companies that have failed to perform in the past or to entities that have unhealthy books or owe back taxes.

Similarly, agencies will frequently require both character and client references. If you're asked for character references and you can give a reference that happens to be a legislator who doesn't mind picking up a phone and vouching for you, well, that's even better. Someone checking your references may be shy of actually calling an elected official to check in on you but being able to honestly list them as a reference sure does make a bold statement, especially if that legislator happens to sit on the committee that funds that agency or department.

Next, never underestimate your competitors – especially in the government marketplace. Whatever you're doing, you can be sure they have either already done, they are doing currently, or will do shortly. I cannot tell you how many times I have been hired because my new client discovered that their competitors hired a lobbyist and they feel the need to "keep up with the Joneses."

Your competition isn't stupid. They know that you entered this game so that you can recruit allies or gain a competitive edge. They know that having a legislator on your side is a huge advantage. They also know that having worked with and received grants and contracts from a government agency gives your company validation and credibility. When you go to ask for that next round of venture capital, having sold your widgets to the DOD holds a lot of weight and may have elevated you above your competition. After all, how many companies can say that the DOD or the U.S. Department of Energy has invested in their technology because they believe in it so much?

In a case where competitors are in the same legislative district, the elected official will likely not be able to choose supporting one constituent company over another. But at a minimum, you've at least neutralized the competition by making the legislator aware of your existence.

In the end, remember you have to be in the game to play the game, and once you're in the game, doors begin to open. But the government sandbox has its own set of rules and expectations.

Final Thoughts on DIY

There are many times when people set out to lobby for themselves and fail. I can't tell you, over the course of the past 12 years, how many clients, for which we've written a proposal, have stolen the ideas and gone out to do the work themselves. Nine times out of 10, they fall on their faces and come back six months later asking us to do damage control.

Don't get me wrong, it is completely possible to do your own lobbying; it's not rocket science. Some people are political by nature and are very well suited to lobbying. Those people understand the game and generally tend to succeed. But if you're the CEO of your company, you need to carefully weigh the options. Is your time better spent building your company or working the issues that surround your company? It's up to you.

That said, I would not be a credible entrepreneur if I didn't end this chapter with a sales pitch. There are countless people like me who have spent years of their lives learning the machinations and nuances of the process to help people like you succeed. If you are still on the fence whether To DIY or Not To DIY, give us a call. We can probably do whatever it is you need faster and more efficiently, but that's your decision to make.

CHAPTER SIX:

The Do's and Don'ts of Lobbying

The Do's and Don'ts of Lobbying

Much of what I am going to tell you in this chapter will seem like common sense. Trust me, lobbying horror stories abound, and you'd be surprised at how many people make silly mistakes – like bringing a weapon to the Capitol. Here are a few basic tips for lobbying success.

The Do's

Always be positive. When giving your presentation, you want to leave your audience with only the positive. If they are opposed to your position, the goal is to get them to move on your request, even if the best you can get from them is a commitment to remain neutral. If you react in a negative way to their position, you may underscore what they already believe.

Remember, if you can show them the impact to the issue at hand, there's a better chance that they'll move closer to supporting your issue. It may be incremental, it may take some time, and they may vote against you for several years, but the idea is to educate them on your position. If legislators or staffers challenge you, it's okay to answer their questions even if they disagree. There are ways of scoring points without being argumentative and to make your point anyway. Remain professional and respectfully disagree when appropriate.

And sometimes silence is golden. Do not engage in unprofessional name calling; you never want to burn a bridge, so being positive and respectful is critical. They'll remember you and your issue, and they'll reach out when they're willing to compromise.

Be willing to compromise. Many times you'll find out there are ways that you can compromise a bit on your position, appear diplomatic and still win the day for your issue. At GSP, we once worked in Washington for the Industrial Resource Centers (IRC) Network of Pennsylvania, a trade association with a handful of members from across the state that received $106 million annually from the U.S. Department of Commerce.

The Network had seven members that shared in a portion of this $106 million (with other IRCs around the country) and with that funding served hundreds of manufacturers in the state of Pennsylvania. Their mission was to support the manufacturing community by linking them to federal contracts and subconsultants to the primes in D.C., guiding them through best practices and ISO certification, making loans to manufacturers that were improving their facilities, and training and retraining the manufacturing workers in Pennsylvania to operate more efficiently.

At the time, there was a fundamental disagreement about the value of this program's funding on an annual basis between Congress and the Bush White House. The Bush Administration didn't like the program as they found it to be unnecessary spending and would always zero out the funding on an annual basis. However, Democrats and Republicans in both the House and Senate overwhelmingly supported it.

GSP was retained by the Network to help lobby Congress and the White House on the value of keeping the funding. This work included, most importantly, lobbying my old boss, Senator Santorum. Santorum at one time supported the program and then eventually changed his mind for a variety of reasons and started to vote against it annually.

When we engaged, we immediately began to work with Santorum and his staff to regain their support. This didn't come quickly. In fact, the first two years of trying were for naught, as the Senator voted against the funding in back-to-back years.

But in year three, we won him back.

In the end, Santorum not only voted for the funding but also worked with other leaders in Congress to raise the $106 million annual allocation to $110 million when our contract had ended. In this example, Rick was the one willing to compromise. If a legislator can bend, keep in mind that you can as well.

Practice makes perfect. With our clients, we put the time in to make sure they are prepared. If you're doing this yourself, you need to prepare for your own meetings. It's very important to know the simple things like, who will be the lead speaker in the meeting with the elected official? If more than one of your team or coalition will be attending, which parts of the argument will each speaker cover?

This is where common sense rules. If one of your team members has an established relationship with the Congressperson or Senator, then that person should be the lead speaker.

I would also recommend a dry run before your meetings or schedule on the Hill begins. Go through your speech in front of your team or, if you're going alone, in front of the mirror. If you've prepared a PowerPoint presentation, be sure to practice the PowerPoint. Get your presentation as close to perfect as you can. These are "Type A" personalities and the people you're dealing with on the Hill are for the most part very intelligent and frequently knowledgeable about a variety of topics, including your own. They will likely know more about your bill than you but you are the expert on your industry. It's often hard to tell a Type A person that they're wrong, but if you can convince them to listen to your side of the issue, smart people will listen. Just remember, everyone gets nervous, which means that practice and preparation are your best friends.

Rallying vs. protesting. The difference between rallying and protesting is the same as using positive or negative influence. Protests are bridge burners. If I show up with a bullhorn yelling and screaming about something, it's guaranteed to turn people off, and it's definitely not going to get the legislator's vote on your issue. Instead, hold a rally in favor of something, like "Please support XYZ issue." You're significantly more likely to get a legislator's attention with a positive approach, than through a noisy, negative campaign.

Let me give you one example. When I was in the district office of Senator Santorum, we were protested by a state union in the heat of a very sticky, very humid summer. The union protestors gathered themselves on Grant Street in the heart of Pittsburgh and with signs, chants and bull horns proceeded to march to the Federal Building to protest us on an issue of import to their members.

Unfortunately for them, the Senator's office was not located in the Federal Building but was in fact in the complete opposite direction across the river in Station Square. Recognizing their mistake, the union march only intensified as they hurried back across the town in the blistering heat, building up a considerable froth, both physically and mentally.

When they arrived in Station Square, much to their chagrin, they learned that the facility that housed our office was on private property and their only recourse was to yell up at our building from the bridge and street below. After 30 minutes of enduring bullhorns and business disruption, security asked us to visit with a small group of protestors so that they could disperse and business could return to normal.

The leaders of the group quickly came up on the elevator and when the doors opened, the bull horns began to blare and chants of "No Justice, No Peace," echoed through our office. They demanded an audience with the Senator only to discover he was on the floor of the Senate in a debate so they decided to compromise and settle for getting him on the phone so they could air their grievances.

I called our press secretary at the time, Tony Fratto, and with one hand over my ear to deaden the bullhorns and chants I yelled into the phone their demands. Tony, uninformed on the issue asked the simple question, "what are they protesting us for?"

At that point, I realized I wasn't really sure. The group had disrupted the office and the businesses around us for nearly 30 minutes and stopped traffic on the bridge requiring police to encourage them back onto sidewalks. So I put Tony on speakerphone and let the group leader weigh in.

When he spoke, we realized he was protesting an issue that was a state-level issue and not a federal one, and again, we had to tell him, “Sorry, we are a federal Senate office and you are protesting the wrong guy. We have no oversight on your issue.”

To say this was embarrassing for him and his perspiring colleagues would be an understatement but after a spectacle like this, did they ever believe the Senator would take their issues seriously again? That is, in part, why protests have the opposite effect of what is really intended.

In contrast to this, one of the best demonstrations we ever received was organized by a local social justice nonprofit organization asking the Senator to not cut school lunches for low-income children.

This issue struck home with me because my brother Dave and I had received free and reduced lunches, among other government benefits, growing up as kids. We grew up in an era where the steel mills had all but closed and even middle income school districts like Baldwin-Whitehall had a significant number of children receiving this benefit. My father was one of those out-of-work steelworkers and even a nickel of assistance helped.

However, this rally wasn’t as altruistic as it appeared; it was just staged in the right way. Behind the rally was a group that was asking Republican offices not to vote for “cutting” the federal school lunch program. What was at hand was a seven percent increase that President Clinton wanted and the Republican alternative was a four percent increase.

That’s right – an increase.

The increase in the program's growth was less than what this group wanted so they spun the message as a "cut." However, what they had done to deliver that message was even more clever.

The group had collected over 1,000 individual paper plates that had been decorated in crayons and markers from kids that benefitted from the program imploring the Senator to not "cut" the program. Messages like "please don't take away our lunches," or "I like my Mac and Cheese," were scribbled in marker on the hand-delivered plates.

On the backs of the plates were the kids' home addresses where we could respond to their parents and tell them if we were voting for the seven percent increase or "the cut."

There were no bullhorns. There were no chants. There were no sweaty protestors disrupting the peace and stopping traffic on a bridge.

Instead, we had a peaceful demonstration done well and delivering a message in a way that I will never forget. And although we disagreed with the message, they had their day with the Senator. In the end, even though he voted against them on this issue, he learned about their cause and voted for them on other related matters in the future.

Rule of thumb drive. One of our little tricks is to put your PowerPoint presentation on a thumb drive. You'll never have a chance to show it to your legislator because you'll typically only get five or 10 minutes with him or her while they are walking down the hall, but you can give your thumb drive and your white paper to their staffer. Also, have something that directs staffers back to your website. That way, if they have follow-up questions, they can either find the answers there, or from there they can find you.

Keep in mind, however, some levels of government have "gift" restrictions and thumb drives may exceed that limit. Some states in which we have operations have limits as low as $4.00. Yes – four bucks. The value of the thumb drive, mouse pad or other trinket you leave behind may accidentally put you in violation of lobbying laws. Be aware of these limits and if they are in place where you will be lobbying, make copies of your presentation as your leave behind material.

Speak their language. Be smart. Be concise. Get to the point. Make sure you're not droning on about your budget and what this will mean in terms of your bottom line. Instead, talk about what's important to them. "Congressperson, this is going to create 50 jobs in your district." Or, "it's going to retain 250 jobs because we have to help this company get over this gap; you will be helping Welfare-to-Work moms get back to work, etc., etc." Every legislator is different, so figure out what's going to motivate him or her; learn their language and use it to your best advantage.

Send a thank you note. As simple as it sounds, sending thank you notes is very important. I personally like to send handwritten notes to people I have worked with on a project. These are very important people who don't have a lot of time to spare, so thanking them for the time they've given you is critical and will help them remember you. And don't just stop with the legislator.

Send a note to the staffer, too. If you can't manage a handwritten note, then send an email. The advantage of an email is that it's instant. The good thing about a handwritten note is that is that it's highly personal, and I would recommend penning it on your company letterhead so it makes you more memorable.

Lobbying is a contact sport; campaigns try to touch each voter three times before an election. Apply the same three-hit logic to lobbying so a legislator becomes familiar with you, your company and your issue. First it's the meeting, second it's the leave-behind whitepaper and thumb drive, and third it's the thank you note.

The memory game. Forging relationships is a big part of lobbying. I have hundreds of people's birthdays recorded in my calendar. I can rattle off the names of legislators' wives, their children and sometimes even their dogs. I will know that your son's soccer team won the state championship, or that your daughter just graduated from college. I will ask how the rest of the family is doing as well. It's this attention to detail that brings about interaction; showing you care by remembering personal details will ultimately make you more memorable.

Make an offer. At the end of a meeting, always offer the legislator a standing invitation to visit your facility. Even it's 2 p.m. on a Sunday afternoon and you have to cobble together a group of employees, board members, or investors you do what you need to do in order to facilitate such a visit. The legislator will get to meet your employees, or if you are a nonprofit, the constituency you serve.

Say you're the symphony and you have a program that raises money to give musical instruments to 200 at-risk kids, you can say, "Look Senator, the school district can't afford to give these instruments to these kids, so this is the good that our organization is doing, come have a look." The legislator takes time to pop by, and the 200 kids go home and tell their parents they got to shake their Senator's hand. It's great publicity for the legislator and for your program. So offer that invitation, even if they can't get over to see you for six months, so that you're on their calendar and it's another point of contact.

In the end, the elected official will remember you and the folks he or she visited. It will enhance your chances of securing their support for a grant or legislative assistance down the road.

Can I get back to you on that? Questions will invariably come up during your meetings on the Hill. Don't expect that you'll have an answer for every question, and don't be afraid to say, "Can I get back to you on that?"

When you follow up, do so in writing as this can be a part of your thank you note. Be sure to reiterate the question asked so as to jog their memory. Remember that your job is to educate them, so the more they know about your issue, the better.

Be early. Promptness matters. In a best case scenario – be early. Worst case – be on time. Legislator schedules change on a dime, and they can get called to the floor for a vote at any time. If they're in leadership, they're getting pulled in 27 different directions. Sometimes legislators have to be at subcommittee hearings and they're scheduled to be at a full committee hearing on something else at the same time. They can't be everywhere. If you're not there, a legislator will skip over you and move right along to the next person in line, to the person who is there.

When they schedule a meeting with you, it is usually for 15 minutes. When the legislator shows up, you will be told, "You've got 15 minutes." Sometimes that 15 minutes really means that you've got six minutes in the hallway and we're going to walk and talk on the way to vote on something. Walk, talk and hand your prepared pieces to the staffer. Be sure to get a business card and a way to follow up. It's a crazy environment and your time is limited, so use it wisely.

Group mentality. If possible, take a small, very focused group of people with you. If your company or organization represents a number of facilities in your state, take the faces of those facilities. Keep in mind, however, that the offices are usually small and that sometimes you're meeting in a foyer or hallway, so you can't bring 10 or 12 people. Think small, and mission critical. There will be times for bigger crowds during rallies, Hill days or when they visit you back in the district or state.

Snack attack. Things are crazy on the Hill, so I always tell people that if they can sneak in a snack, do it. Never turn down a chance to get something to eat or drink or, for that matter, to use the restroom. You might get pulled into a meeting, or the Senator you're waiting to see is held up on the floor. You never know when they're going to take a break, and you don't want to be buying a bag of Chips Ahoy when that happens. You need to stay put and wait, because you might not get another chance if you're off roaming around scrounging the premises for something to snack on. So take snacks with you.

I was walking with a client from one meeting to another; my upcoming meeting was with a majority leader of the Pennsylvania State House. It was a busy day of session, and the only reason we got in to see him was because of his relationship with our Harrisburg team. I warned my client, "Look - he's going to walk out of his office, stop, and shake hands in the foyer. He's going to continue walking to the way to the House floor where he's going to vote, and they're going to close the doors behind him because you're not allowed in there. You've got 10 minutes – maybe six if he walks fast – because in all likelihood he is going to be late."

Right then, my client says, "I have to pee."

I am not sure what my face looked like at that moment, but I am sure my countenance held an awkward smile. It's not often you hear a grown man in a tailored suit mutter, "I have to pee," but that just happened.

Before I could even react, one of my Harrisburg lobbyists, Stacy Gromlich, blurts out in the most serious tone, "No - you can't pee."

She said it loud enough and authoritative enough that everyone in the room heard it and chuckled, but was serious enough that the client got the picture.

I know. It sounds comical, but every word is true. Bear in mind that you are only going to get your sliver of time when it's available to the elected officials, and they won't wait for your potty break.

Don't overlook the district staff. It's tempting to go straight to the top of a legislator's office or to the legislator directly if you can. Since the center of power in most legislative offices is in Washington or the State Capitol, you intuitively make that junket to get yourself as far up the food chain as possible. Perhaps you can even find your way into a one-on-one conversation with the legislator themselves at a public event. These things can all help but they can also backfire if you don't play your cards right.

Most legislative offices rely on a team of local or "district" staff representatives to serve as the first line of defense and opportunity for constituent-driven projects, causes, and problems. Some offices have even institutionalized this chain of command, so when you contact the "Capitol" office, you will get pushed back to the district team no matter how strong your Rolodex.

Process, however, is not the main reason for engaging the district staff, early and often, in your lobbying activities.

First, district staffers are often as approachable and responsive as their Capitol Hill peers. Because fewer people think to start their campaign this way (and because many people don't even realize legislators have district staff), these assets often go underutilized.

The district staff members are also tasked by their boss to find promising projects and causes to support, so when you reach out to them proactively, you are actually making their jobs easier. You should be able to not only get a meeting in their office but even get them to visit you on your turf, to do a tour of your facility, or meet with your employees.

Secondly, district staffers often have the same levels of access to the legislator, as well as to government agencies and other legislative staffs, as their Capitol counterparts. If you find a district staffer who really likes your project or cause, they can become your own lobbyist within the organization, opening doors that your paid lobbyist often can't.

You will also find that there is less turnover in a district office, while Capitol offices are often a revolving door. This means that a long-tenured district staffer might just have better contacts and deeper institutional knowledge of the game than the staffer with the prestigious Senate Office Building address on Pennsylvania Avenue.

Lastly, district staffers are just as important to your cause as are the Capitol Hill staffers.

Now, I'm not suggesting that district staff can get your project or cause through the bureaucratic labyrinth on their own or that you shouldn't take that meeting with the Chief of Staff or Senator when you can get it. But, engaging the district staff in your campaign from the beginning and throughout the process can prove extremely valuable for what amounts to a minimal investment in time and resources (it beats shelling out money for airline tickets and hotel rooms on K Street.)

Make your message about them. I'm sure your company has invented the most amazing new technology in the world and that your legislative issue is the most important cause your Congressman can take up this year. Every legislator and staffer on the planet hears hyperbole like this from virtually every constituent that walks in their office. While your claims may indeed be true, an office-holder has only so many priorities they can tackle in the two, four, or six years they have until their next election.

To get your initiative the kind of attention you want, you need to be mindful of the goals and priorities of the legislator sitting across the table from you and craft your message in a way that resonates with them. As you form your story and collateral materials, ask yourself these questions: What were their biggest campaign promises and priorities when they ran for office? How does your project line up with those promises? Will you help to create jobs in their state or district, save lives, reduce government waste, or improve the environment? Tie your work in some way to the betterment of their district and you will win their hearts and minds.

The Don'ts

Weapon free zone. Never come to the Capitol with a weapon of any kind. This seems like a no-brainer, but at least once a year, one of my clients will forget that there's a Swiss Army knife, or a wrench, or a flashlight on their keychain. They're hunters or fishermen, and they just forget. They might be an off duty policeman who's used to carrying a firearm, or a woman who carries pepper spray in her purse. Whatever is it, do a personal inventory before leaving the house and make sure you're weapon-free.

Let's face it, it is better not to be detained by Capitol Police than getting pulled aside and asked why you are carrying a weapon in to see a legislator.

One hand doesn't wash the other. Never equate an official meeting with a legislator with something you did for them. For instance, if you made a contribution to a campaign or held a fundraiser for them, you can't bring that up in a meeting. You didn't get the meeting based on that effort. The legislator is meeting with you for reasons that are completely separate from whatever it is you did for him or her.

People who don't lobby professionally often make this mistake. Regardless of what you've done in the past, rest assured that the legislator will know and remember; it needn't be discussed in your meeting.

One time I was in a meeting with about 40 others to meet with then U.S. Senator Arlen Specter. The meeting was about President Clinton's universal health care coverage bill and there were about five interested groups that were coming in to visit the Senator to discuss his vote. Arlen, ever the moderate Republican, was on the fence on this bill and hadn't decided how to vote. I was there as a staffer for Senator Santorum and wanted to hear the group position on the bill.

The meeting started with one of the leaders thanking the good Senator for his time and then he launched into a quick reminder for the Senator that he and three other gentlemen in the room had met with Arlen the week before at a fundraising event.

Arlen stood slowly and interrupted the gentleman by saying, "I am sorry but I cannot sit in this meeting now," as he and his staff left the room.

A hush fell over the room and there was sufficient embarrassment for everyone. The Senator did the right thing by pulling himself and his staff out of a situation that could have been misconstrued. As innocent and "rookie" as the mistake was, the group leadership had committed a cardinal sin in their lobbying effort and there are no "Mulligans" in lobbying.

Don't wage a personal war. As a DIY lobbyist, you are going to sit in on a lot of meetings with legislators and staff. Some will be great and some not so great.

If you feel that a meeting isn't going as well as you'd hoped, be silent. It doesn't matter if the legislator was insulting and you've now decided to vote against the legislator, just refrain from telling him or her that. You can think it, but don't let the words come out of your mouth. The minute you cross that line, you are threatening that person, and everything falls apart. You can discuss it later with your team and say, "That guy was a jerk." While this is part of the democratic process, and you're entitled to that opinion, just keep it to yourself until you're far away from the legislator. There will be time to address it with their leadership or during the next election.

No protests. I mentioned this in the "Rally Do's", so it goes both ways. Stay away from protests. People respect rallies and peaceful demonstrations if you keep it positive. As soon as you organize a protest, you burn bridges and turn people away from your cause or issue.

Never lie. As mentioned earlier, questions are bound to come up that you cannot answer or are ill prepared to answer. Whatever you do, don't lie. Don't make something up to just answer the question because staff will fact-check the information you give to them.

When a legislator goes to vote on your issue, he or she is going to need the correct information. Remember, you can always follow up with answers to their questions when you send your thank you note, but lying on the spot to avoid looking uniformed always comes back to haunt you. Legislators know you will likely not have all the answers but are willing to wait to make sure they have the right answers so they can accurately decide how to vote.

Don't be nervous. If you've never been to D.C. and you feel like you're going to be really nervous, go a day early to acclimate yourself with your surroundings. It's easy to feel intimidated when you walk into the halls of Congress with its vaulted ceilings, gorgeous domes, and important-looking people walking around with purpose in suits. People think, "What am I doing here. I'm just a simple Joe, I own a coffee shop and I'm here on behalf of the National Association of Businesses, and even though they asked me to come here, I don't feel like I belong."

Admittedly, the D.C. environment can be daunting, but legislators like meeting people, talking with them and trying to help them. Just because you may see them on television doesn't mean that they are completely different from you. They are your advocates, and they are there to work on your behalf.

Feel free to get there a day ahead and map out your routes between buildings and meetings. In D.C. your group can even request (through a friendly legislative office) the use of a room in the new Capitol Visitors Center, conveniently located between the House, the Senate and just outside the Capitol itself.

If you reserve a room, you can have legislators and their staff come to you instead of you fumbling through the halls and walls of the Dirksen Senate Office Building. You can also have the rooms catered for you and your traveling companions as well as for visiting legislators.

Don't be star struck. This isn't the time to ask for an autograph or personal photo. Legislators are people too. While they are important people, they are people nevertheless, and typically they'll send you a letter of thanks, which is suitable for framing if you're so inclined. Perhaps you'll go to a fundraiser and you can have your picture taken then. So don't embarrass yourself, stick to the business at hand, and be professional.

In short, be smart, use your common sense and prepare for all potential outcomes. None of these Do's and Don'ts will ruin a good, solid lobbying campaign. But being on your game is your best line of defense when navigating the political process.

CHAPTER SEVEN:

The Last Chapter is the Next Chapter

All good entrepreneurs enter business knowing one day they will exit that same business. When they do, they want to find the perfect partner with which to deploy that exit strategy. In our case, GSP found that perfect partner in the most unlikely of places – a law firm.

I know, I've just spent a hundred pages explaining why our business model is superior and that law firms with lobbying practices are commonplace in our business. So why would this business that prided itself on being different exit into the very competitor that it railed against since its inception?

The answer was simple. We had a chance to take GSP to the next level and grow it at an order of magnitude greater than we could have taken it on our own. We owed it to our employees and clients. If we could stay true to our founding principles while enjoying some of the benefits of being associated with a prestigious legal house it would be a grand slam.

In the spring of 2011, GSP was approached by Duane Morris, an international law firm headquartered in Philadelphia but with 24 offices, domestic and international. The initial foray had been made by Duane Morris through one of their government affairs directors, Eric Martins. Martins was longtime friends with GSP's Philadelphia Director, Ted Christian, and the two advanced the conversation of a possible merger of GSP and Duane Morris Government Affairs (DMGA), a wholly owned subsidiary of the law firm.

At first blush, I have to admit to a level of disinterest. The entire philosophy of GSP was founded to be different than what was commonplace in our market. How could a merger between the rebel GSP and the epitome of the establishment, DMGA, ever work? In this case, opposites attract.

The merger talks advanced and in the summer of 2011, a turning point was reached in the conversations when our leadership team finally met in person with the Duane Morris leadership team in Philadelphia. My guard was raised but my interest was piqued.

The meeting between the sides initially rambled through discussions about what they do best and why we thought this might be a good fit. We realized shortly after the conversations began that the core competencies of both firms were the same, but that each firm possessed strengths that the other did not. I would have to credit the Chairman and CEO of Duane Morris, John Soroko, for simplifying the initial conversation. He summed up the value proposition of the merger eloquently by stating "if we do merge, we eliminate each other's weaknesses on day one and double our areas of strength."

When we were on our flight home, Amy and I looked at one another and couldn't disagree. In the proposed merger, the two firms would double the size of our D.C. and Harrisburg practices while adding to each others practices in Minnesota and Ohio from GSP and New Jersey and Maryland from DMGA. GSP would enjoy a PAC that was five times as large as our GSP PAC and DMGA would inherit several new service offerings like grant writing, procurement, grassroots lobbying and development finance consulting. These were new services DMGA couldn't provide to their customers pre-merger and if we played our cards right, we could start marketing these new services to a self-contained sales funnel of 20-plus law offices scattered around the globe. Where was the downside?

Sitting silently on the short flight home, I couldn't conjure up a reason not to do this.

When my business partner and I first hung out our shingle, one of our goals was to create a different kind of lobbying firm. You know the story now - I'd been lobbied. I'd seen the good, the bad and the ugly from the other side of the table. John and I wanted to do something different.

So, armed with our respective Rolodexes, John and I set out to make a difference in the way things were done. We wanted to represent a group of people that traditionally didn't have lobbyist representation. We targeted technology companies because we knew we could reach them on a variety of levels. Those companies also fell into the small-to-medium niche markets. We also targeted trade organizations and nonprofits – those municipalities that couldn't afford the fees associated with the big lobbying firms, but that still needed representation and advocacy.

We saw a flaw in the system and we seized it as an opportunity. We had influence with people, but we didn't want to use influence peddling to get things done. Instead, we wanted to sell the commoditization of our domain expertise.

You need help writing this grant? You need help writing this Request for Proposal? You need help with the parliamentarian aspects of changing a policy that affects your business or your industry? We're going to help you do that. We're going to help you figure out how to stop a bill, how to tweak a bill, or how to get legislators to champion something. We set out to do that for companies in a way that our competition had either ignored or didn't want to endeavor. The beauty of it was that we had a target-rich environment and no one else wanted to play in it.

And now we stood on the precipice of merging this professed better mousetrap into an entity that represented the antithesis of what GSP stood for. How can I do that?

Trust.

I have to admit, our team was won over by the honesty and trustworthiness of our new partners. Soroko was as honest as the day was long. He and his COO, Charles O'Donnell believed in the model we had built so much that they wanted us to team with their partners to raise the combined entity to the next level. They wanted to see us take our combined strengths of team and methodology and roll it out under the new banner internationally. We were their first-round draft pick. And it felt right.

DMGS

Over the past ten months, the leadership teams of the former GSP Consulting and DMGA came together to create Duane Morris Government Strategies, or DMGS. DMGS has become a culmination of the strengths of each of its predecessors. The new entity is equally likely to serve a Fortune 100 company as it may two guys in a basement that just spun their new tech company out of a university. It is a unique blend of an international law firm incubating an entrepreneurial consultancy with goals of quadrupling its size in the next five years. All in all, it's like starting a new business again - but this time with a big brother.

So the end of one chapter leads to the exciting beginning of another, and I am humbled to be given the chance to lead this great combined team to new heights with my new business partners and employees.

Since the merger, I have been asked multiple times about whether I would do it again. And although I am sentimental and nostalgic about closing the doors of GSP, the spirit of my old company lives on in the fabric of DMGS.

One of my best friends, Kent Szalla, once told me that "beer is only as good as the people you drink it with." And although those words were mumbled after sharing a case of Old German in college, they have more wisdom in them than first meets the eye.

What he meant is that regardless of what you are doing, the experience of it is only as good as the people you share it with. And my team, both former and new, are the ones with whom I want to share in this renewal and opportunity.

CONCLUSION:

Checkmate

As I stressed earlier, lobbying is a lot like a game of chess. In order to checkmate your opponents you will need to divine a little better than they do and anticipate the moves your competitor is going to make next.

In Washington, that is much easier said than done. There is always someone on the other side of the table trying to get what they want, which in many cases can be in the exact opposite direction of what you want to accomplish.

When you hire a professional like a GSP or a DMGS, you naturally gain both immediate subject matter expertise and the depth and breadth of the teams' combined networks and the Rolodexes. Working with the government isn't nearly as scary as people think. The government can even be a positive partner if you know what you're doing and if you do it well. Just remember that the government can be both a primary and secondary marketplace with opportunities for non-dilutive funding and a phenomenal place to sell products and services.

So if you can't afford to hire a professional lobbyist, simply follow the principles enumerated in this book and learn from the case studies and anecdotes I provided.

Please do understand that there's a firm whose guiding philosophy has brought lobbying to the masses, and made government accessible to niche groups that were previously underserved. It's available to you if you need that level of service. So hire us, or do it yourself, but understand that simply identifying what you need is the first step. Then work the steps until you accomplish your goal – whether it's funding, a policy change or something else entirely. Develop a comprehensive government strategy that will work for your organization and launch a plan of action to get you to the next level of business success. It's just that simple.